T0090337

ALSO BY GEORGE MCGOVERN

The Third Freedom: Ending Hunger in Our Time

*Terry: My Daughter's Life-and-Death Struggle
with Alcoholism*

War Against Want

Grassroots: The Autobiography of George S. McGovern

The Great Coalfield War (with Leonard Guttridge)

*An American Journey: The Presidential Campaign Speeches
of George McGovern*

A Time of War, a Time of Peace

Agricultural Thought in the Twentieth Century

Our Founders and the Liberal Tradition

THE
ESSENTIAL
AMERICA

★ ★ ★ ★ ★ ★

GEORGE
McGOVERN

★ ★ ★ ★ ★ ★ ★

Simon & Schuster

New York   London   Toronto   Sydney

SIMON & SCHUSTER
Rockefeller Center
1230 Avenue of the Americas
New York, NY 10020

Copyright © 2004 by George McGovern
All rights reserved,
including the right of reproduction
in whole or in part in any form.

SIMON & SCHUSTER and colophon are registered trademarks
of Simon & Schuster, Inc.

For information about special discounts for bulk purchases,
please contact Simon & Schuster Special Sales at
1-800-456-6798 or business@simonandschuster.com

Book design by Ellen R. Sasahara

Manufactured in the United States of America

1   3   5   7   9   10   8   6   4   2

Library of Congress Cataloging-in-Publication Data is available.

ISBN-13: 978-0-7432-6952-0

To my parents, Frances and Joe; Eleanor's parents, Marian and Earl; Olive and Larry; Ila and Bob; Pete, Harry, and George; and to our special friends, Ward Clark, Bill Towner, Joe Floyd, and Steve Ambrose; and, of course, to precious Terry—all of these in the realm of the mystery beyond.

CONTENTS

THE
ESSENTIAL
AMERICA

★ ★ ★ ★ ★ ★

Chapter 1

FAITH OF OUR FATHERS

Those who won our independence by revolution were not cowards. They did not fear political change. They did not exalt order at the cost of liberty.

—SUPREME COURT JUSTICE LOUIS BRANDEIS, 1927

MY FATHER, J. C. MCGOVERN, was a Methodist clergyman—a follower of the eighteenth-century English founder of Methodism, John Wesley. A fierce opponent of slavery and an ardent defender of the poor and unfortunate members of society, Wesley had a stronger following in the slums and sweatshops of London than in the castles and country estates of the realm. A proponent of personal salvation, he was equally committed to what a century later was called "the social gospel." He believed that the Judeo-Christian ethic called upon believers to demonstrate compassion for the homeless, the sick, the vulnerable, and for the miners and factory workers. As one biographer noted, "Wesley was passionate about the need to alter economic policies that encourage greed and punish the poor. He was an advocate of lowering taxes and reducing the national debt by minimizing military spending." (Ronald Stone, *John Wesley's Life and Ethics,* Abingdon Press, 2001)

Following his death, in 1791, England's widely read *Gentleman's Magazine,* whose editorial views were not always compatible with Wesley's thinking, observed: "His personal influence was greater perhaps than any private gentleman in this country." His biographer concluded that "Wesley made the most rational and persuasive arguments against slavery of any person in the 18th Century."

Wesley's social conscience and his message of individual salvation were brought by Francis Asbury to early America, where he found eager recipients.

George Whitefield, the English fellow Methodist of Wesley and Asbury and a powerful pulpit orator, came to America in 1739 in the first of a series of visits to the colonies. Utilizing the revival meeting technique first employed by Jonathan Edwards, he preached to large open-air crowds, drawing multitudes of listeners from virtually every religious denomination. His appeals to personal salvation given in highly emotional language shook up the established churches and in the early 1740s set off "the Great Awakening" of spiritual concern throughout the colonies. The messages and articles by Whitefield gained broad circulation after being printed by a young Philadelphia printer, Ben Franklin. Despite his then meager income, Franklin reportedly said that he found it difficult to avoid giving all that he had to Whitefield.

No one who overlooks the moral and spiritual views of our founders can fully grasp the enduring strength of American freedom. Who were the founding fathers? Perhaps no two historians would suggest the same list of the personalities who led the thirteen colonies to independence from Britain and then shaped the new American nation. Here is a suggested list:

Tom Paine, the author of *Common Sense* and a passionate advocate for the revolution against British rule, who aimed his message at the ordinary American; George Washington, the commander in chief of the revolutionary armies and the first president of the United States; Thomas Jefferson, the author of the Declaration of Independence, who crafted his prose to appeal to the most educated and influential Americans and to the ruling class in Europe, whose help was needed in the American Revolution; Benjamin Franklin, who presided over the convention that drafted the Constitution; John Adams, the sturdy voice of conservatism and the nation's second president; James Madison, Alexander Hamilton, and John Jay—the three brilliant authors of *The Federalist Papers,* designed to persuade the American people to adopt the Constitution; Samuel Adams, a powerful advocate of American independence; Patrick Henry, Virginia's eloquent orator and supporter of independence; Roger Sherman, a member of the Continental Congress and signer of the Declaration of Independence, the Articles of Association, the Articles of Confederation, and the federal Constitution—the only person to sign all four of the major state papers; Gouverneur Morris, signer of the Articles of Confederation, member of the Continental Congress, financier and U.S. senator from New York; James Wilson, member of the Continental Congress, delegate from Pennsylvania to the Constitutional Convention, justice of the U.S. Supreme Court, and first professor of law at the University of Pennsylvania; and John Hancock, president of the Continental Congress, first signer of the Declaration of Independence, and first governor of Massachusetts.

From its beginning, American democracy has been grounded both in the Judeo-Christian ethic and in the European Enlightenment—with a generous seasoning of down-home common sense. What was the Enlightenment that so heavily influenced our founders?

The Enlightenment was the revolutionary trend of thought that appeared in Europe and the American colonies during the eighteenth century. Writers and thinkers of the period believed that humanity was emerging from long centuries of ignorance, superstition, darkness, and misrule into a new age of reason, science, and respect for the individual. Descartes, Spinoza, Hobbes, and Locke were seen as the forerunners of the age, followed by Newton, Kant, Montesquieu, Diderot, Voltaire, Rousseau, Hume, and, in the United States, Jefferson and Franklin.

The Enlightenment thinkers placed emphasis on the power of human reason, disciplined by experience and observation. They came to believe that through education, humanity could be changed for the better. Most of the Enlightenment figures did not renounce religion, but they were sometimes critical of the doctrinaire, authoritarian nature of the established church. They generally opted for

Deism—a faith in God but not in every aspect of Christian theology. Jefferson edited his own Bible, which consisted only of the words of Christ. He and other Deists tended to encourage a better way of life on earth rather than hopes for the hereafter. Without exception they respected the moral law—if not always the proclamations of the organized church and the theologians.

The voices of the Hebrew prophets, the teachings of Christ, and the thinking of eighteenth-century European philosophers are all clearly present in the messages of Thomas Jefferson—the author of the Declaration of Independence; James Madison—the chief author of the Constitution; George Washington—the "father of his country"; John Adams—the early conscience of conservatism; and, of course, Abraham Lincoln—who saved the Federal Union and emancipated the slaves. Others, including Tom Paine, Benjamin Franklin, and Alexander Hamilton, were more skeptical of spiritual faith. Even Jefferson rejected some parts of Christian theology and a literal reading of passages of the Old Testament. But all of these men accepted the centrality of the moral law as a necessary guide to government and human affairs.

Later presidents, including the two Roosevelts, Woodrow Wilson, John F. Kennedy, and Jimmy Carter, drew inspiration and guidance from biblical verse. In President Kennedy's intended speech in Dallas on that fateful day—November 22, 1963—he quoted the biblical lines "Except the Lord keep the city, the watchman waketh but in vain" (Psalms 127:1). He concluded another address with these words: "Here on earth, God's work must truly be our own."

• • •

Our founders believed in what they repeatedly referred to as "the moral law" or "the natural law"—terms that they used interchangeably—as did such European thinkers as John Locke, David Hume, George Berkeley, Voltaire, Rousseau, Montesquieu, Descartes, Kant, and John Stuart Mill. Jefferson combined the natural, moral, and spiritual—referring to them as "the laws of nature and of nature's God."

Jefferson, Madison, and Franklin were especially influenced by Locke's belief that natural law "hath brought men to know that it is no less their duty to love others than themselves. . . ." Here, of course, is the "golden rule" of the Bible. In another passage, Locke refers to the rule of "a common reason and equity, which is that measure God has set to the actions of men, for their mutual security. . . ."

One of the most cherished legacies of our founders is the separation of church and state. It was Jefferson who used the phrase "a wall of separation." Under attack today by the religious Right and a significant number of the Supreme Court justices, it remains a safeguard against manipulation of the state by the church or the church by the state.

In the eloquent opening lines of the Declaration of Independence, Jefferson contends that "the laws of nature and of nature's God" entitled the American colonies to independence and freedom from British rule. But in later years his concern over some of the failings of the American Republic, especially the practice of slavery, led him to confess: "I tremble for my country when I reflect that God is just." Jefferson's troubled mind did not, however, prompt him to release his own slaves. Only Washington among the founders took that step.

The Americans Jefferson most trusted and admired were the farmers who tilled the soil. "Those who labor in the earth are the chosen people of God, if ever He had a chosen people, whose breasts He has made His peculiar deposit for substantial and genuine virtue," he wrote.

Circling the dome of the magnificent Jefferson Memorial at the Tidal Basin of the nation's capital are these words by the Sage of Monticello: "I have sworn upon the altar of God, eternal hostility against every form of tyranny over the mind of man."

Always worth repeating are his ageless words in the Declaration of Independence: "We hold these truths to be self-evident, that all men are created equal, that they are endowed by their Creator with certain unalienable Rights, that among these are Life, Liberty and the pursuit of Happiness." Reading these stirring lines, Lincoln said: "I have never had a feeling, politically, that did not spring from the sentiments embodied in the Declaration of Independence." The Declaration, he said, "gave liberty not alone to the people of this country, but hope to all the world for all future time."

George Washington was not as expressive a man as Jefferson or Lincoln, but none doubted his moral integrity or his reverence for the things of the spirit. Consider these words as he addressed his army before it went into the Battle of Long Island on August 27, 1776: "The fate of unborn millions will now depend, under God, on the courage and conduct of this army."

Lincoln, regarded by many historians as our greatest president, was the one who drew most heavily and consistently from the Bible and spiritual faith—perhaps because the endless agony and destruction of the bloody Civil War drove him to his knees. It should be noted that in his limited education, Lincoln never read a novel, nor did he read the classics with which Jefferson and others were familiar. But he was immersed in the King James Version of the Bible, as well as the legal commentaries of Blackstone and, to some extent, the works of Shakespeare.

Speaking to an audience in his home state, Illinois, in 1858, Lincoln inquired: "What constitutes the bulwark of our own liberty and independence? It is not our frowning battlements, our bristling seacoasts, our army and our navy. . . . Our reliance is in the love of liberty which God has planted in us. Our defense is in the spirit which prized liberty as the heritage of all men, in all lands everywhere."

Quoting the Gospel According to Mark (without attribution), Lincoln declared: "A house divided against itself cannot stand."

In his farewell address to the citizens of Illinois before assuming his duties in Washington as the nation's newly elected president, Lincoln said on the eve of the Civil War: "I now leave with a task before me greater than the one which rested upon Washington. Without the assistance of that Divine Being who ever attended him, I cannot succeed. With that assistance I cannot fail."

Lincoln's tendency to probe the depths of the spiritual as a means of lifting the hearts of his fellow citizens—North and South—is seen in his First Inaugural Address, as Civil War clouds were gathering force:

"The mystic chords of memory, stretching from every battlefield and patriot grave to every living heart and hearthstone all over this broad land, will yet swell the chorus of the Union when again touched, as surely they will be, by the better angels of our nature."

As the war gained greater ferocity and destruction, with Negro slavery emerging as the central issue of the conflict, Lincoln told a visiting delegation to the White House: "It is difficult to make a man miserable while he feels he is worthy of himself and claims kindred to the great God who made him."

A year later, November 19, 1863, Lincoln delivered his brief but powerful address at Gettysburg, in which he concluded that "this nation, under God, shall have a new birth of freedom—and that government of the people, by the people, for the people, shall not perish from the earth."

In his final inaugural address, as the Civil War was drawing to a blood-soaked finish, Lincoln reminded his listeners that each side prayed to the same God for victory, but that obviously both sides could not prevail. "The Almighty has His own purposes," he said.

"Fondly do we hope—fervently do we pray—that this mighty scourge of war may speedily pass away. . . .

"With malice toward none, with charity for all; with firmness in the right, as God gives us to see the right, let us strive on to finish the work we are in; to bind up the nation's wounds . . . to do all which may achieve and cherish a just, and lasting peace, among ourselves, and with all nations."

Were the early architects who crafted a nation from thirteen British colonies along the eastern American seaboard men devoted to organized denominational religion? In almost every instance, the answer is no. Were they saintly men, free from the lusts of the flesh and the sins that plague the rest of us? Certainly not. Were their personal lives and private practices always attuned to the soaring moral and political principles they publicly proclaimed? Not always.

The noble Jefferson, whose inspired rhetoric has lifted the vision of his fellow Americans for two centuries, was a slaveholder throughout his life. It is widely believed that one of his female slaves was his mistress and the mother of one or more of his children. Benjamin Franklin was the author of a much-quoted letter: "Advice to a young man on the advantages of an aging mistress." Conceding that the complexions of older women are sometimes wrinkled, he noted that their thighs remain smooth and inviting to the end. With an older mistress one need not fear an unwanted pregnancy. The final asset of such an older companion, according to Franklin, is that "they are so grateful."

To read the definitive biographies of our founders is to discover that few, if any, of them, despite their inspired thoughts and elements of greatness, escaped the snares of the devil who tempts all of us. My father was fond of the words of the Apostle Paul: "All of us have sinned and come short of the glory of God." That's certainly true of me, and I believe it applies to the founders of our nation and all of their successors.

But with these reservations in mind, there is a strong recognition in the prose, poetry, and pronouncements of our founders from Jefferson to Lincoln of the moral and ethical law that derives from the King James Version of the Bible and the philosophers of the European Enlightenment. Islam and the other religions of the Orient had not yet made an impact on the Western mind. But it is clear that our founders not only knew the wisdom and spiritual insight of the Bible but drew heavily on the European thinkers—especially Locke and Montesquieu, Rousseau and Voltaire—and later, John Stuart Mill.

No one who aspires to lead this nation into an uncertain future in war or peace should undertake that daunting task without drawing on the time-tested moral and political principles of our founders—liberty, equality, justice, truthfulness, and compassion for all of God's creatures everywhere.

The battle cry of my 1972 presidential campaign was "Come Home, America"—a call for the American people and our government to come home to the founding principles of the nation. This was a phrase borrowed from the fallen Martin Luther King Jr., after my wife, Eleanor, discovered it in one of his eloquent sermons.

Of course, political leaders have always appealed to legitimate traditions and insights apart from the faith and wisdom of our founding fathers.

Bill Clinton, who performed brilliantly in 1972 as my campaign coordinator for the state of Texas, was himself the Democratic presidential nominee in 1992. With remarkable skill, he then defeated the senior President Bush with a campaign slogan: "It's the economy, stupid." Apparently, it *was* the economy that concerned most voters. But I think it is important to understand, as I am sure Bill Clinton does, that the economy is a means to an end—not an end in itself.

An economy is no better or worse as an instrument of national policy than the wisdom and integrity of those who direct it.

Consider, for example, the German economy of the 1930s. Adolf Hitler achieved a productive, prosperous, full-employment economy that was the envy of an otherwise depression-ridden world. But he used that economy for barbaric ends. He directed his associates to build the world's most devastating military machine and then smashed his way across Europe until he was finally stopped on the vast steppes of Russia by the huge Red Army. Twenty-two million Russian soldiers and civilians—many of them children and teenage army lads—died in that awful struggle, but so did 6 million German soldiers before the Russians prevailed on the eastern front as our superb soldiers, sailors, and fliers did on the western front and then against Japan.

What was the missing ingredient in Hitler's scheme? Certainly not the economy. It was the total lack of any moral sense as to how the political leadership and the economy could be put to the service of the people. One cannot measure the terrifying brutality and immorality of Hitler, his powerful economy and his mighty war machine, without considering his slaughter of 6 million innocent Jews—a major part of them his own citizens and most of the others citizens of Poland and Russia. It is shocking to realize that Hitler was able to debauch morally and intellectually a nation that had given the world Goethe, Beethoven, Thomas Mann, Albert Schweitzer, and Albert Einstein. In this case, it was not the economy that was the problem. It was the deterioration of simple old-fashioned decency and the rudiments of morality.

Thirty years later, Presidents John Kennedy and Lyndon Johnson guided America to a prosperous, growing economy, with President Kennedy calling the nation to a "New Frontier" and President Johnson dreaming of a "Great Society." But these vigorous, strong presidents became enmeshed in the Vietnam quagmire. As a consequence of that awful miscalculation, much of the idealism and hope for a better future died, along with our bravest young men, in the jungles of Southeast Asia that had swallowed other would-be conquerors for a thousand years. Sadly, we set aside the wisdom of Washington, Jefferson, Lincoln, Wilson, and Roosevelt and embarked on a misconceived venture ten thousand miles from our shores—and equally distant from our national ideals.

I'm a supposedly combat-hardened bomber pilot of World War II with thirty-five missions against Hitler's most heavily defended targets, but each time I walk along the Vietnam Memorial's black marble wall carrying the names of 58,000 young Americans who died in Vietnam, the tears course down my cheeks. I think also—and then shudder in the knowledge—that 2 million Vietnamese, 2 million Cambodians, and 1 million Laotians—5 million of God's Asian children—died in the Indochina conflagration largely as a result of the massive, misdirected military power of my great country. I quote Jefferson again: "I tremble for my country when I reflect that God is just."

There are two consoling factors in this tragedy: (1) ours is a forgiving God; and (2) it is quite possible that the terrible lessons learned in the jungles of Southeast Asia saved us from vastly greater losses had we gone to war against Russia and China—the real centers of Communist power. No Russian or Chinese soldier fought us during our long involvement in Vietnam, but the world's two biggest armies were out there watching and waiting to see if our troops and bombers were going to trespass across their borders.

Writing in 1942, as the United States was entering World War II, Herbert Agar, one of our brilliant social critics, observed: "The savages who assail us may teach us to re-examine our faith, to review the greatness of our tradition, to remember that we have not done it justice." And again: "Such plagues as Hitler are not irrelevant to history, like falling stars. They happen only in bad times, in a world whose institutions are failing to meet the demands of life."

As Agar concluded eerily in World War II: "We have learned in grief what happens to a world that strays too far from its moral purpose." (*A Time for Greatness*, 1942, pp. 4–6)

As I reread these lines written six decades ago, I think of our present assailants, Osama bin Laden and his Al Qaeda network of terrorists. Of course, the American people and our leaders were understandably traumatized by the murderous attacks of September 11, 2001. They have dominated our politics and our foreign policy ever since—much as the fear of communism did between 1945 and 1990.

President George W. Bush quickly announced: "I want Osama bin Laden dead or alive." But after our heavy bombers had turned Afghanistan into a rockpile, we failed to get Osama bin Laden and his top henchmen either dead or alive. Nor, despite our superior weapons and the smashing of ancient Baghdad, has our superb army been able to find any weapons of mass destruction—the supposed reason for the invasion of Iraq. Now the men and women of our occupying army are being picked off daily by Iraqi guerrillas with no end in sight—shades of Vietnam.

Is it possible that preponderant military power and earthshaking aerial bombardment are not the best antidotes to the terrorist zealot? It is past time to ask ourselves some hard questions. How is it possible for a wealthy Saudi Arabian Islamic fanatic, Osama bin Laden, to move through the slums of Cairo, the hills of Afghanistan, and the backcountry of Saudi Arabia and recruit other disgruntled Muslim zealots willing to die striking at the world's richest and most militarily powerful nation? Our president says these young men are cowards who hate American freedom. I respectfully disagree with that interpretation. I think I can assure you as a former pilot that flying a plane into the side of a huge building knowing that the pilot will be the first to die is not the work of a coward. Misguided? Certainly. Cowardly? Hardly.

Nor do I believe the young men of Al Qaeda hate our freedom. I think what they more likely hate is the miserable and frustrating condition that afflicts their neighbors in the rural villages and city slums of much of the world. Insufficient food, bad housing, no sanitary water, little or no medical and dental care, few or no satisfying jobs—and now the terrible epidemic of AIDS. Moreover, half the people of the planet are living in poverty. These heart-rending facts were known and observed year after year, day in and day out, by the somewhat more comfortable and better-educated young men who flew the hijacked airliners of 9/11. These young men were not blind to the miserable living (or dying) conditions of their poorer compatriots. They also knew that the Western countries, including the United States, where some of them were educated, are living on a scale—sometimes of great extravagance—beyond their dreams. In some instances, their own regimes are ruled by high-living royalists closely tied to Washington and London in trade, investment, oil, and military aid that keep those unpopular regimes in power.

And mingled with despair and misery is the incendiary impact of religious fanaticism. The Middle Ages and even early modern Europe were racked by bloody religious wars. Human beings are capable of terrible acts when driven by spiritual zealotry, as we are witnessing again in our time.

I am convinced that it is the misery of their own people, contrasted so painfully with our lifestyles, that thousands of young people around the world deeply resent. I have found the same kind of dual resentment in Latin America—resentment of their conditions of life and resentment of the colossus of the North. Indeed, I have yet to visit a country anywhere in the world whose rank-and-file citizenry supports the American invasion of Iraq, our embargo of Cuba, and our tight embrace of Israel. These aspects of American policy are seen by others as arrogance and insensitivity toward the world community. This, of course, is no reason to hijack our airliners and destroy the lives of innocent Americans.

But neither can we dismiss the frustration and fury of these angry young men by branding them as cowards who hate our freedom. That is simplistic reasoning that will achieve little in reducing the growing resentment against America—not only in the Arab world but even in Europe and our neighbors in Latin America, to say nothing of such large states as Russia, China, Pakistan, Indonesia, India, and the whole suffering African continent.

I suspect that the public opinion surveys that show world approval of our government declining to new lows do not indicate that this stems from our freedom; rather, it derives from the arrogance and go-it-alone character of too much of our foreign policy and national political behavior. The crass, heavy-handed reputation of the current administration has been fed by such actions as the spurning of the Kyoto Protocol to reduce global warming—a danger to our future that is matched only by the proliferation of nuclear weapons. Likewise, our government's unilateral withdrawal from the Anti-Ballistic Missile Treaty with Russia and instead pressing ahead with the so-called Star Wars missile defense system in space does not build the stature of America abroad. It is, in fact, a mistaken move, both diplomatically and in terms of security. The same can be said of our government's rejection of the International War Crimes Court. Both our national prosperity and our international standing sink lower each time our president talks of an American military invasion. It is painful for us to contemplate, but in many countries, America is viewed as a "bully" and a threat to peace among nations—especially the current administration's neocons' doctrine of "preemptive war."

Ponder Herbert Agar's words of 1942 again: "The savages who assail us may teach us to re-examine our faith, to review the greatness of our tradition, to remember that we have not done it justice."

Joseph Nye, the dean of Harvard University's John F. Kennedy School of Government, who is also a former Defense Department official, has concluded: "Anti-Americanism has increased in recent years, and the United States' soft power—its ability to attract others by the legitimacy of U.S. policies and the values that underlie them—is in decline as a result." (*Foreign Affairs,* May/June 2004, p. 161)

We can fill our airports with police officers, security experts, and searchers of our luggage—even taking off our shoes to be examined. We can create the biggest and most expensive security bureaucracy in the world and call it "Homeland Security." We can legislate the misnamed Patriot Act, which weakens the Bill of Rights. But we live in a world where millions of people are frustrated, angry, and desperate over the conditions of their lives. Do not these intolerable conditions feed the flames of terrorism? Suicide bombers, grenades, or dynamite sticks thrown into American theaters, restaurants, shopping centers, or buses can easily become a reality, no matter how powerful our military forces. Israel has one of the most effective armed forces in the world and one of the tightest national security systems, plus an experienced general as prime minister. Yet each time Israeli troops, tanks, and planes have fired on Palestinians, a Palestinian youth burning with revenge becomes a suicide bomber, and another group of Israelis is blown to pieces.

Can we find a better way of dealing with Iraq, Iran, Syria, Lebanon, Sudan, Afghanistan, and North Korea, or even tiny Cuba, and other countries and leaders with whom we have disagreements? I have never been a pacifist. There is a time and place when the use of military power may be the only effective option, as it was in facing down Hitler and his Axis allies. But there are crucial problems in the world that cannot be reached by military solutions. Such a problem, I believe, is terrorism.

The decade-long international embargo against Iraq contributed to the deaths of untold numbers of Iraqi children. Many women and elderly poor have also suffered from the embargo, combined with the poor leadership and brutality of Saddam Hussein.

But does anyone really believe that sending our army into Iraq is going to reduce the terrorist danger to the United States? The nineteen young men who wrecked the World Trade Center and the Pentagon came not from Iraq but from Saudi Arabia and Egypt. Their leader was not an Iraqi but a Saudi, residing in Afghanistan. What has engaged the Iraqis in terrorism has been the presence of our army in their country. And the victims of this new terrorism are our young soldiers, who have been killed at an average rate of fifty each month since President Bush announced in May 2003 "Mission Accomplished" in Iraq.

It is immoral to invade a comparatively defenseless country and kill its people because they have the misfortune to be ruled by a ruthless dictator who our war strategists speculate might someday be a threat to us.

The Iraqi people know that our strategists backed Saddam Hussein as long as he was killing Iranians in the 1980s, just as we backed Osama bin Laden and the Taliban in Afghanistan in the 1980s as long as they were killing Russians.

If we really want to use our power and influence effectively in the Middle East, we would be well advised to concentrate our creativity and our political and moral strength on ending the suicidal conflict that has raged for generations between Israel and the Palestinians.

Neither Palestinians nor Israelis can resolve their differences militarily. Israeli tanks and jets and Palestinian suicide bombers will not decide this deadly contest. They can only run up the cost in lives lost on both sides. A moral sense of decency and reality on the part of the Israeli and Palestinian leaders, and on the part of the United States as the logical moderator, might bring peace at last. If we are to play that role, we have to do so in a just and even-handed way. The late Israeli prime minister Yitzhak Rabin understood these realities and shook hands with Palestinian leader Yasser Arafat at the White House to cement that understanding in the presence of President Clinton after vigorous and successful effort by Mr. Clinton.

One of the most costly assassinations in history was the

murder of Rabin by a deranged Israeli religious fanatic who opposed a peaceful settlement with the Palestinians. The peace process has been in trouble ever since, which the killer intended in murdering one of its essential architects. I believe that our president is too obsessed with the "axis of evil," as he calls it—Iraq, Iran, North Korea—and with Syria, Lebanon, Somalia, and Sudan, all designated by the Bush team as having regimes that may have to be removed by American forces because of alleged sanctuaries for terrorists. (Elizabeth Drew, *The New York Review of Books,* June 12, 2003) If, instead of a preoccupation with these small and nonstrategic countries, the president would give top priority to settling the Arab-Israeli conflict in an even-handed approach, he would not only serve the cause of peace and justice but might even reduce the terrorism of the Middle East. It has never been a case of one side being "right" and the other "wrong." In a sense, there are two "rights"— Israel's right to live as a free and independent nation within secure borders, and the Palestinian right to an independent, secure state situated on the West Bank of the Jordan River and the Gaza Strip, the territory taken from the Palestinians in the 1967 Six-Day War.

From the creation of the state of Israel in 1948, we have armed and equipped the Israeli military until it became the most powerful armed force in the Middle East. Israel long ago built a nuclear arsenal that strikes fear into its Arab neighbors. I have always regarded myself as a friend of Israel and an admirer of its cultural, political, economic, and spiritual traditions. My Methodist minister dad honestly believed the Israelis were "God's chosen people." But the only way we can now help Israel survive in peace and security is to press the peace process as a truly honest broker. This is not only the honorable, moral role for us to follow; it is the only one that may lead to peace at last in the troubled Middle East. For the benefit of both Israel and the Palestinians, this is the goal I hope and pray we Americans can help to advance. Anything less than this even-handed posture will be rejected by the Palestinians and the Arab world, and the violence will continue.

Americans and our leaders must come to understand that terrorism is driven not only by poverty and injustice, but also by the long-festering Arab-Israeli conflict over the unresolved Palestinian problem. Most influential Arabs and the leaders of nearly all of the nations of the world believe that the dynamite on our doorstep is planted by the daily violence between Israel and the Palestinians. The Israelis in the period since 1967 have built large numbers of settlements on the occupied territory, which, of course, is the nub of the problem.

Every informed Arab knows that U.S. administrations, Democratic and Republican alike, have from the creation of Israel in 1948 usually sided with Israel in any dispute with the Arabs. Repeatedly in votes at the United Nations, Israel and the United States have stood alone against the wishes of the world. The United States has frequently used its veto power to block UN resolutions opposed by Israel—most recently the UN resolution condemning Israel's assassination of the Palestinian leader of Hamas.

I have long supported Israel. But after years of study and observation of Middle Eastern affairs, I have concluded that such hard-line Israeli leaders as Ariel Sharon—the current prime minister—and earlier, Benjamin Netanyahu, are a menace to Middle East peace. Neither of these men has enjoyed approval in the international community. They are despised by Arabs everywhere. And as their backer and arms supplier, the United States becomes the target of Arab ire. We ignore that anger and resentment at our peril.

There will be no progress against Al Qaeda and terrorist Islamic cells such as the one suspected of the Madrid train bombings until the Israeli-Palestinian conflict is resolved. That is the long-festering antagonism that feeds the terrorist impulse in the Arab world.

Beyond the tensions of the Middle East lies a world in which half the inhabitants long to be emancipated from the bonds of hunger, poverty, illiteracy, and disease. Some of these miserable ones are Americans. The United States cannot alone relieve all these burdens that crush our fellow humans. But we can show the world an American face of compassion.

Everyone understands that we are the richest and most powerful military nation in human history and that we would, if necessary, use that power to defend our country. But our greatness began with a small band of remarkable men who followed "a faith that could move mountains," even the mighty British Empire. To advance that faith, they pledged their lives, their fortunes, and their sacred honor.

To us, as comparatively affluent Americans, the number one problem seems to be terrorism. One has the impression that the White House, the Department of Defense, the CIA, the FBI, and the State Department are working around the clock on nothing save the terrorist threat. Even the misguided invasion of Iraq has been sold to much of the American public as a "war on terrorism." The truth is that Iraq has not waged any attacks on the United States and was no threat to Americans until the president ordered our army into Iraq. This occupation has infuriated much of the Arab world, and brave young Americans are dying as a consequence.

To most of the people in the Middle East, Asia, Africa, and Latin America, the central problem is not terrorism; it is poverty combined with injustice. This is the combination that produces the desperation which drives the terrorist impulse. When we add to this anger and desperation our government's longtime embrace of Israel, the terrorist danger grows for both Israel and the United States.

What steps could the United States take that might be a more successful response to the terrorist challenge?

(1) First, we should remove our army from Iraq, where our soldiers are now being killed and wounded in an inconclusive guerrilla-type war that Western armies are not able to manage very well. Most of the Arab world, including those who detested Saddam Hussein, is against a foreign army occupying the heart of that Arab world. Indeed, if we can believe the public opinion polls, the overwhelming majority of the world's people everywhere are against our invasion of Iraq. This is true even in the few countries whose heads of state endorsed the war. It may soon become true of

the American majority if our casualties and financial costs continue to escalate. As soon as we can turn Iraqi governance back to representative Iraqi groups, let's get our army out of the Middle East.

(2) Second, let us replace our unilateral, isolationist foreign policy with one that cooperates with the United Nations, our traditional allies, and the other countries of the world. As the late senator George Aiken once said of our predicament in Vietnam, "Let's declare victory and come home."

We should join the Kyoto Protocol on global warming and support the International War Crimes Court and the ban on land mines. Instead of putting weapons into space, we should halt this costly program and concentrate our efforts on checking the proliferation of nuclear weapons here on earth.

(3) Third, we should toughen our stand on the necessity of ending the bloody tit-for-tat killing going on between the Israelis and the Palestinians. This bitter contest over Israeli settlements on the West Bank of the Jordan River must stop before it destroys both Israel and Palestine. Palestinians will apparently never yield their claim to this land, which they believe should be the space for an independent Palestine. The Israelis seem equally determined to defend their settlers living in the disputed area.

As I write, the Israeli leader Ariel Sharon has proposed a unilateral initiative endorsed by President Bush under which Israel would give up the Gaza Strip to the Palestinians— a desolate piece of ground that no one seems to want. Sharon also proposes to exchange some of the West Bank settlements for other areas of settlement.

It was a mistake for President Bush to endorse this Sharon proposal without consultation with the Palestinians. As one would have expected, the proposal was dead on arrival among Arabs and has since been rejected by Sharon's own party.

The only way for the United States to proceed as a Middle East peace moderator is to bring the two leaderships together, as President Jimmy Carter did at Camp David and as President Bill Clinton did later, and keep them talking until a compromise settlement is reached. I have long been convinced, as have most of the world's leaders—including some prominent Israelis—that the only workable solution is for Israel to withdraw from all of the land taken in 1967 and permit the Palestinians to create there an independent Palestine. If there is a foreign minister or head of state anywhere in the world who disagrees with that solution, I have yet to encounter that person in long years of extensive travel.

The United States has poured billions of dollars into the development and defense of Israel. We continue to do so. We will stand on solid ground—historically, politically, and morally—if we now insist that continued aid is contingent upon a just and lasting peace.

It would be a bargain for the United States to join with the United Nations in providing an international police force along the Israeli-Palestinian border to stabilize such a peace agreement. This arrangement could last for ten or fifteen years, or until such time as it takes for the Israelis and the Palestinians to discover that they are all human beings—indeed, they are all Semites, they all live in the Holy Land, and they are all children of the same God.

It might be wise for President Bush (or President Kerry) to name former presidents Bush Sr. and Carter to preside over the peace negotiations between the Palestinians and the Israelis. These two experienced men know the complexities of Middle East issues. They also know the pressures in American politics that frequently dominate our foreign policy. Both have a record of diplomatic success: President Bush in handling the run-up to the Gulf War in 1990 and President Carter in the Camp David accords with Israel and Egypt.

A solution to the Arab-Israeli conflict will do vastly more to end the terrorist threat than sending our army into Iraq.

(4) A fourth step to reduce terrorism would be a substantial increase in the food, medical, educational, water, and housing aid from the wealthy countries to the poor ones. UN agencies such as the World Food Program and the Food and Agriculture Organization—both located in Rome—are well situated to manage this kind of aid, but they need additional funds. Careful programming of assistance can do much to ease the misery and desperation that breed terrorism.

I'm not much of an expert on anything—except the St. Louis Cardinals. But I have thought long and hard about three major problems: how to bring America's policies closer to our founding ideals; how to end the hunger of the world's poor; and how to bring peace to the long-troubled

Middle East. There are people who know better than I how to get the Cardinals into the World Series. There are others who know better than I how to make America more faithful to its founding ideals, or how to end human hunger, or how to resolve the turmoil of the Middle East.

What you have here are the thoughts of one aging ex-senator who yearns for American greatness and peace in the world—and a pennant for the Cardinals. The last of these may be impossible this year, so I'll settle for a great America and a world at peace.

For most of my public years, including the 1972 presidential campaign, what I have most longed for is to see America once again become the great and good land it can be when we are faithful to the ideals of our founders. That is a pursuit that might energize conservatives as well as my fellow liberals. We should be able to make room in heaven for those conservatives who at long last see the light!

Chapter 2

THE SPOILS OF WAR AND THE FRUITS OF PEACE

Professional soldiers, including members of General Staffs, tend to be cautious, conservative and unadventurous.... Hyperpatriotic fire-eaters, moreover, are more common in most modern States among businessmen, petty burghers, and political demagogues than among aristocrats, generals and admirals.

—FREDERICK L. SCHUMAN,
INTERNATIONAL POLITICS, 1948

WITH THE COLD WAR ending in 1990, the time is past due for our government to declare a peace dividend for the benefit of the American people. During the half century of Cold War between Washington and Moscow, with its enormously costly arms race, our strategists embraced what was called "the 2½ war" doctrine. That formula called for the United States to build and constantly upgrade a military force that would enable us to fight and win wars simultaneously with the two major Communist nations, Russia and China, plus one smaller country such as North Korea or oil-rich Iraq or Iran. The military budget was established at a level equal to the estimated cost of the two-and-a-half-war theorem. Decade after decade, from 1941 until today, the Pentagon has claimed the biggest portion of federal spending. Most of our taxes have gone to the Pentagon since 1941—especially during World War II, the Korean War, the Vietnam War, and now the Iraq war. And the so-called neoconservatives who are highly placed in the Bush administration have plans ready to go for half a dozen additional wars if Mr. Bush is given a second term.

During all these years, the American people have been told that because of the Russian-Chinese danger, these mammoth expenditures were necessary to safeguard our security. Anyone familiar with my record in the Senate during the 1960s and 1970s knows that I never totally bought this line. I always favored a strong national defense, but I firmly believed that a sky-is-the-limit policy on military spending weakened rather than strengthened the country. Such needless spending placed an excessive burden on taxpayers, drove up the national debt, and deprived us of funds for other sources of well-being such as national health care for every American.

I tried every year to reduce the Pentagon budget. All of these efforts, although of modest proportions, were rejected by the Senate in considerable part because of two factors: first, every senator had one or more defense installations in his or her state that provided jobs for that state's voting constituents. The second factor was even stronger—senators were reluctant to give a demagogic opponent an opening to brand them as weak on defense.

No matter how many boondoggles were added either by the administration or the Congress to the Pentagon budget, that budget would sail through the House and Senate intact. Senators who argued heatedly for days over a comparatively small appropriation for education, health care, or job training would approve the gigantic military outlays with a whoop and a holler.

Anything carrying the label "defense" was considered sacred and untouchable. Who would want to take even a few dollars away from "national defense"? Better to *add* dollars to the defense bill, which was done regularly every year. I once considered offering an amendment to the military appropriation bill to reduce it by one dollar, but I decided that would trivialize the issue and, of course, it would have been voted down, lest the Russians consider we were going soft!

One senator who stood up regularly on this issue, a close friend, was the former governor of Wisconsin, Gaylord Nelson. I have known many good men and women in public life and a few great ones. Gaylord is both good and great, and his delightful wife, Carrie Lee, is a special national treasure. Gaylord, who watched our failing efforts to amend the military bill and our inability to force an end to the mistaken war in Vietnam, began to vote against the entire military appropriation. That took courage. But, as Gaylord told his constituents, "Wisconsin can get a new senator; I can't get a new conscience." At least in part because we were falsely branded as "weak on defense," Gaylord, Frank Church, John Culver, and I were all defeated in 1980. We were all veterans of the armed forces with distinguished war records. No one of us would ever cast a vote against the security and well-being of the nation.

Why did I work so hard to reduce military spending? Because I knew, as would any open-minded person who looked at the facts, that both we and the Soviets had twice the killing power needed to pulverize the other side. This was the modern-day "balance of power"—the doctrine of mutual assured destruction, or as the fitting acronym put it, MAD. Once this level of destructive power was achieved, roughly around 1960, each side could literally wipe out the other nation, no matter which one struck first. In the event of nuclear war, once the Soviets and the Americans were incinerated, large parts of the populations of other nations would die of radioactive fallout carried by the winds from the blackened ruins of the deceased superpowers. Needless to say, there would be no victor in such an act of madness or miscalculation.

Many times during the half century of Cold War rivalry between Washington and Moscow, our alert systems identified what was believed to be an oncoming USSR nuclear attack. In each case, it proved to be a false alarm, thus saving us from mistakenly firing our missiles targeted on the Soviet Union. Had we launched such a salvo, the Soviets would doubtless have responded, and the final war of the world would be decided in a few minutes, with no prisoners, no survivors, and no victors.

In August 1945, we dropped two nuclear bombs on Japan, eliminating two modern cities and their populations.

A nuclear war between Moscow and Washington could have seen twenty thousand nuclear warheads exploded—each more deadly than the two that hit Japan and brought it to its knees.

Thank God that neither we nor the Soviets were willing to engage in this unprecedented orgy of suffering and death—perhaps the death of our planet.

There were always a few people in our midst urging a preventive nuclear strike against the USSR and China. Doubtless, similar urgings were offered in Moscow. We can be grateful that such lunatics never came to power in either the United States or the Soviet Union. If they had, I would not be around to write this book and you would not be around to read it.

Repeatedly during the Cold War the American people were told that if we could find a way to end the arms race with the USSR, there would be a peace dividend. In other words, if we were freed from the costly burden of an open-ended arms contest, the military budget could safely be cut, with the savings diverted to constructive purposes. This vision began to emerge as a reality with the coming to power of Mikhail Gorbachev as president of the Soviet Union in 1984. A former minister of agriculture and a brilliant man, Gorbachev had a strong feeling for his people, for their land, the working families, the rich cultural traditions, and the vast resources of Mother Russia. He saw the folly of continuing the waste and the incredible danger of an open-ended arms race with the United States—a vastly richer and more modern nation than Russia.

In 1986, in a conference at Reykjavík, Iceland, he discussed these views with President Ronald Reagan. To his credit, President Reagan welcomed Gorbachev's views. The two men tentatively agreed that *all* nuclear weapons should be abolished. They then turned the matter over to their advisers and arms experts, who worked out a considerably more modest agreement for staged reductions of nuclear arms. But the arms race was reversed, however modestly.

Some have said that Gorbachev made his proposal because of Reagan's buildup of America's armed forces and his plan to build an anti-ballistic missile system in space—the so-called Star Wars idea. I am more inclined to think that Gorbachev was acting from his own commonsense conclusion that an endless superpower arms race was not in the interest of either side. That, of course, was what he said at the time and what he has repeated to numerous visitors, including me. If he had wanted to secure a Soviet gain at our expense, he doubtless would have welcomed the Star Wars fantasy as an ideal way of wasting billions of American tax dollars on a worthless piece of military hardware—just as the Soviets had sometimes done because of their fear of our escalating war machine. I have yet to meet a nuclear scientist who believes that extending nuclear weapons into outer space will make America more secure.

In any event, the Cold War ended more than a decade ago and the arms race, involving the USSR, China, and the United States, is halted. Russia stands alone, with the fourteen other former Soviet states now independent countries. The Eastern European countries that were previously tied to Moscow—Poland, Czechoslovakia, Hungary, the Baltic

States, Romania, Bulgaria, and East Germany—are now free and independent, with East and West Germany reunited. For its part, China has emerged as a "most favored nation" trading partner of the United States.

No sensible person any longer believes that our military budget should be set to fight major wars simultaneously with Russia and China, plus a minor country.

So where is the peace dividend? There have been a few reductions in Pentagon spending, but nothing of major consequence. No other country is threatening us—certainly not Russia or China or our enemies in World War II, Germany, Japan, and Italy. Some are worried about Cuba or President Bush's "axis of evil"—Iran, Iraq, and North Korea. But that is a pretty meager shopping list of potential enemy states. What rational person believes that any one of them would attack the United States unless we decided to attack them first, as we did Iraq in 2002, North Korea in 1950, Cuba in 1961, and Vietnam?

Our current arms budget is roughly $500 billion, including the annual cost of the war in Iraq. That is greater than the combined total of all military spending of the rest of the world. No nation has ever before had such a preponderance of military force. Our fleet encircles the globe with aircraft carriers, battleships, submarines, and planes with bases everywhere—some three hundred at last count. Our war planes and missiles can strike any part of the globe. The U.S. Army, U.S. Air Force, the Marine Corps, and the U.S. Navy are the best-equipped and best-trained fighting forces anywhere on the planet. We have a superb officer corps in all branches of service. Every time I have visited American military units across the United States and around the world, I have been highly impressed with the training, equipment, and dedication of our armed forces. America has never had better officers and servicemen and -women than the ones we have today. I thought my comrades were pretty tough fighters in World War II. Today's forces are every bit as good, and in some respects better, because of improved physical health and superior, unhurried training. I'm especially proud of my eighteen-year-old granddaughter, Marian, a member of the U.S. Air Force. It pleases me that she joined my old service branch, but I hope she doesn't feel bound to become a combat pilot!

In 1942, at the age of nineteen, I volunteered for the Army Air Corps to become a bomber pilot. This was shortly after the Japanese attack on December 7, 1941, against our fleet anchored at Pearl Harbor. Expecting to begin training immediately, I was not called to service for a year. Why? Because the air corps was critically short of training planes, instructors, and airfields. My delayed pilot training began on a dirt field in Muskogee, Oklahoma, with a bush pilot civilian instructor pressed into service, complete with an inexhaustible supply of large cigars that filled the cockpit of our light plane with smoke. Fortunately, despite having no military flight experience, Herb Clarkson was a superb pilot and a demanding instructor, who taught me rudimentary lessons of flying that were to save my life and the lives of my crew on many subsequent missions in aerial warfare abroad.

But the point of all this is that I never want to see America's military defense sink to the level it was when we were faced with the dangers of World War II. On the other hand, I believe with equal conviction that America is weakened by military spending that goes vastly beyond what is needed for defense.

My role model on defense matters is five-star General of the Armies Dwight D. Eisenhower. During eight years as president, 1953–61, including the last months of the Korean War and the building of nuclear weapons by the Soviet Union, Eisenhower did his best to hold military spending in check—not always successfully.

The first time I became interested in trying to bring arms spending under control was when I read the great farewell address of President Eisenhower in January 1961. With the possible exception of President George Washington's farewell address in 1779, President Eisenhower's is probably the most important. Rather than trying to summarize this message, which centers on his concern with the mounting power over our society of "the military-industrial complex," let us look at a few paragraphs of this powerful statement. Interestingly, the two farewell messages that I have identified as the best in our two centuries as a nation were both given by generals who had been promoted to the highest military rank before assuming the presidency.

In his final address as president, George Washington said: "Those who love America will avoid the necessity of those overgrown military establishments which under any form of government are inauspicious to liberty, and which are to be regarded as particularly hostile to republican liberty."

President Eisenhower gained the respect of the world for his leadership in World War II—including that of Field Marshal G. K. Zhukov, the great Russian wartime commander who defeated the legions of Hitler's Germany. He spoke these words at the end of his eight years in the White House while he awaited the inauguration of his successor, John F. Kennedy: "In the councils of government, we must guard against the acquisition of unwarranted influence, whether sought or unsought, by the military-industrial complex. The potential for the disastrous rise of misplaced power exists and will persist."

Having served as president of Columbia University, Eisenhower noted that "the free university, historically the fountainhead of free ideas and scientific discovery, has experienced a revolution in the conduct of research. Partly because of the huge costs involved, a government contract becomes virtually a substitute for intellectual curiosity. For every old blackboard there are now hundreds of new electronic computers. The prospect of domination of the nation's scholars by Federal employment, project allocations, and the power of money is ever present and is gravely to be regarded."

I was electrified by those words—in part because the president had spoken the truth so articulately and in part because, like other Americans, I had long admired him. I wondered then, as I do today, why these thoughtful words from one of our most admired soldier-statesmen did not have a more profound impact on the American government and public opinion.

One possible reason is that John Kennedy, whom I held

in affection and admiration, had campaigned across the nation on a pledge to "get this country moving again," which included, as he saw it, the need to strengthen the armed forces and to close "the missile gap." It was argued by some of our military authorities that the Soviets had moved so far ahead of us in missile production that they had created a "gap" threatening our survival.

The Gaither Commission, a group of wise men appointed to look into this alleged Soviet preponderance of power, leaked portions of the findings of their "secret" study to the press. One unidentified member of the commission said he was so terrified by the Soviet military superiority that he felt as though he had just looked into the jaws of hell.

Kennedy accepted this reasoning and contended that the country needed a more vigorous military. Eisenhower, during his eight years in the White House, was the only president since World War II who fought each year to check arms spending in the face of a rising national debt. This made him unpopular at the Pentagon and with its staunchest allies both within the government and outside.

But Eisenhower was right. Once in the White House, John Kennedy discovered that there was a "missile gap," but it was in our favor. We had more missiles, with greater accuracy, than the Soviets. The advocates of more military spending repeatedly discovered "gaps" in our defense when it came time for another military appropriation—a "bomber gap," a "submarine gap," an "intermediate-range missile gap," a "naval gap," a "tank gap." All of these "gaps" proved to be false. The United States always was well ahead of the

Soviet Union in quality of weapons and overall military strength, to say nothing of our clearly superior economic, financial, industrial, and agricultural power.

During the ninth month of his presidency, John Kennedy came to grips with the nuclear peril. Speaking to the United Nations General Assembly on September 25, 1961, Kennedy said: "Today every inhabitant of this planet must contemplate that day when this planet may no longer be habitable. Every man, woman and child lives under a nuclear sword of Damocles, hanging by the slenderest of threads, capable of being cut at any moment by accident or miscalculation or madness. The weapons of war must be abolished before they abolish us."

In what may have been his greatest speech, the commencement address of June 10, 1963, at American University, President Kennedy announced that he had ordered a cessation of testing nuclear weapons in the atmosphere. The Soviets followed suit, and a few weeks later the two nuclear giants ratified the Nuclear Test Ban Treaty.

Also in 1963, Kennedy approved the sale of American wheat to Moscow. A third step toward improved relations took place that year with the installation of a special direct telephone line between the White House and the Kremlin.

The backdrop for these more peaceful steps was the grim and frightening Cuban missile crisis of October 1962. As Admiral Hyman Rickover put it: "The two superpowers looked into the nuclear abyss and the Cold War can never be the same."

President Kennedy did proceed in the 1960s with his campaign pledge to provide greater diversity and flexibility in our defense forces, including the development of counter-guerrilla special units. Unfortunately, this helped to create the myth that we were now capable of moving decisively into the Vietnam jungles.

But doubtless, the larger reason why Eisenhower's counsel was rejected is that neither the Pentagon nor its congressional allies wanted to hear the nation's commander in chief warning against the increasing power and influence of the "military-industrial complex."

He had an enthusiastic junior ally in me. During my first year in the Senate, and subsequently, I quoted Ike's message in the Senate and across the land.

Years later, at the 1999 dedication of the late professor Stephen Ambrose's D-Day Museum in New Orleans, I found myself seated on the platform next to Eisenhower's top longtime military aide, General Andrew Goodpaster. To my surprise, the general leaned over to me and said softly: "President Eisenhower thought highly of you." I will treasure that bit of knowledge all of my days.

My second major speech in the Senate, "New Perspectives on American Security," was delivered on August 2, 1963. In that speech I called for us to recognize that the Department of Defense was not the only source of American security. A strong, full-employment economy is also a source of American power and security. A healthy, well-educated citizenry provides a vital part of a nation's security. A clean, safe environment is another foundation of strength and national security. The world's strongest, most productive family farms and ranches are another crucial foundation stone in our national security. A credible political leadership with an open, honest political process is a crucial part of our security and influence in the world.

All of these factors contribute to our security and national defense. If the military takes more of the budget than it needs, it weakens the nation by starving these other contributors to national vitality and health.

Every one of the significant issues facing our nation today is at bottom a moral challenge—war and peace, foreign policy, politics, the physical environment, the economy, taxation, education, health care, alcoholism, and drug addiction. No one of these concerns can be adequately addressed without a revival of the spirit and moral sense of the American people and our leaders. This is the faith that guided our presidents from Washington and Jefferson to Lincoln, Wilson, and Roosevelt, as enshrined in the Declaration of Independence, the Constitution with its Bill of Rights, and in their inspired messages to the people of America—especially Lincoln's matchless Gettysburg Address.

At the end of World War II, as I piloted a battle-scarred B-24 bomber homeward across the Atlantic with the survivors of our crew, I felt we were fortunate to have completed thirty-five missions over some of the most heavily defended targets in Europe. Despite the sad memories of comrades lost, I was jubilant on that long moonlit flight home across the ocean. We had won the war.

I exulted in our victories over tyranny and fascism, knowing that our 15th Air Force had smashed Hitler's oil refineries, destroyed his tank and plane factories, and disrupted his major railway marshaling yards. But as I flew over the white, billowing clouds with the moon smiling down on my sleeping crew, my mind drifted to a daughter I had not yet seen, dear Ann, who had been born while I was overseas. My father had died while I was in combat, but now another young life was helping to fill the void. I thought of my dear wife, Eleanor; my mother; my brother and two sisters. And as the night moved on toward dawn, I thought of the United Nations, which, in the words of its chief proponent, FDR, "joined together in war to preserve their independence and their freedom" and "must now join together to make secure the independence and freedom of all peace-loving states, so that never again shall tyranny be able to divide and conquer." (Final State of the Union address, January 6, 1945)

With the two superpowers—Russia and the United States—working together as they had during the war, and with the help of historical allies, including Britain, France, Canada, Belgium, China, Australia, and the Scandinavian countries, I thought, perhaps naively, that the post–World War II world was eager for a century of international cooperation, development, and peace.

But this was not to be. With Germany, Italy, and Japan defeated, Moscow and Washington each decided that the other one was now the chief threat to their survival. Almost before the last shot was fired in World War II, Moscow and Washington launched the Cold War and the most terrifying arms race in human history. For nearly half a century, 1945–90, the two superpowers committed the major part of their national budgets to the strategic arms race. Each side soon had enough nuclear warheads to destroy the other and much of the world several times over, no matter which country struck first. This meant, of course, that neither side dared launch a nuclear attack on the other—knowing that the resulting retaliation would erase them from the global landscape. Fortunately, neither the Soviet Union nor the United States ever fired a single bullet at the other superpower.

Stephen Ambrose, author of a series of highly successful historical works, devoted some of his best research to a two-volume biography of General and President Dwight Eisenhower, which he did at Eisenhower's own request. During this work, he sent me a memo from the files of the National Security Council in the spring of 1960. The memo described a meeting of the council in which the secretary of defense was making the case for more long-range missiles. President Eisenhower interrupted to note that we already had enough intercontinental ballistic missiles (ICBMs) to kill every Russian. That's true, said the secretary, but if we halt production now, the Russians might assume that our will is weakening and would therefore be tempted to attack.

In a moment of disgust, Eisenhower said: "If there is anything to that argument, why don't we build ten thousand of the damn things and be done with it."

That is what was done on both sides—thousands of "the damn things" for us and an equal number for the Russians. Did this enormous buildup make the world safer? Hardly.

Two decades later, President Ronald Reagan pressed for more nuclear weapons, including "Star Wars." Speaking on March 31, 1982, Reagan said: "The truth of the matter is that on balance the Soviet Union does have a definite margin of superiority—even so that there is risk and there is what I have called, as you all know several times, a window of vulnerability." Reagan may have sincerely believed this line, put out by a group calling themselves the Committee on the Present Danger. But the statement was a preposterous falsehood that served the interests only of the military-industrial complex of which Eisenhower had warned. It was good for the profits of our major defense industries; it was not good for the American people.

All during these years, the American leadership, the Congress, and our people lived in mortal fear of Moscow and its allies. This fear not only drove the arms race, it dominated our foreign policy and our budget priorities. At times it distorted and weakened our politics when political figures and writers sought to discredit their opponents by labeling them "soft on communism"—whatever that might mean. I have never met either a Democrat or a Republican who was pro-Communist. I have met a few who were pressing to the edge of fascism. Bloody American wars in Korea and Vietnam were fought largely to demonstrate our anti-Communist resolve. Around the globe we sometimes entered into alliances with brutal dictators who were willing to wave an anti-Communist banner.

Under the intellectually tough, commonsense leadership of Soviet president Mikhail Gorbachev, whose proposals to develop a more peaceful and orderly world met with the approval of President Ronald Reagan, the Cold War began to thaw. Between 1989 and 1991, the Soviet satellite states in Eastern Europe were allowed to shake loose from their ties to Moscow and the fifteen republics of the Soviet Union went their separate ways. The Cold War was over.

I suspect that most thoughtful Americans now know that the nuclear arms buildup of the Cold War was vastly overdone on both sides. Because of the unexpected disintegration of the Soviet Union—at least unexpected by the CIA—many Americans seemed to assume that we won the Cold War. It would probably be more accurate to say that the USSR—much weaker economically, politically, and militarily than the United States—finally fell victim to a flawed economic and political system, plus the exhaustion of trying to keep up with the United States in an openended arms race.

One of the tragic consequences of the Soviet-American arms craze and the Cold War was that they paralyzed the newly launched United Nations organization. The USSR and its allies tended to oppose and, if necessary, veto American initiatives—and the reverse was also true. Seldom did either side cooperate with the other in UN matters. Fear and rigidity dominated foreign policy in Moscow, Washington, and the United Nations for nearly half a century.

Fear and fearmongering have had a long history in America, stretching back to the witchcraft hysteria in colonial Salem, Massachusetts. Fed by the overly active imaginations or down-home paranoia of a small band of teenage girls, a number of Salem residents were accused of witchcraft, tried in court, and executed. When the Reverend Cotton Mather became suspicious of the girls' charges and invited them to his home, once they realized that their stern clergyman was interested only in their souls, they readily confessed to perpetrating a hoax and the executions were halted—but not before an entire community had been traumatized.

In the early years of the new American nation, a different brand of hysteria and fearmongering seized many of our political spokesmen and the American public. In this instance, which resulted in the notorious Alien and Sedition Acts of 1798, Americans were aroused to a frenzy by Federalist politicians who used the fear of the French Revolution and later the aggression of Napoleon to paint vivid portraits of the French menace. Some of the most extreme and fearful warnings of French subversion of America were designed to discredit Thomas Jefferson in the presidential election of 1800. The old conservative incumbent president John Adams had his political differences with the more liberal-minded Jefferson, but the tirades of his fellow Federalists against the Sage of Monticello finally were more than Adams could take.

To the excited cry of one Federalist orator predicting that if Jefferson were elected to the White House, French armies followed by wicked French atheists would take over America, Adams snorted: "I no more expect to see a French army in America than I do in heaven!" The Alien and Sedition Acts were designed to exclude alien penetration of America and made it a crime for Americans to criticize policies of their government.

Other outbreaks of fear and hysteria included the dismal but often brutal and terrifying antics of the Ku Klux Klan. These tactics on the part of racist southerners, but including many northerners, were designed to terrify Negroes and their white sympathizers into submission to racial discrimination and segregation. Racism and its handmaiden, terrorism, were not finally banished legally by the federal government until the great civil rights legislative, administrative, and judicial efforts of the 1950s and 1960s.

Following World War I and the Russian Revolution, America was seized by another brand of terrorism—a wave of anti-Communist hysteria—the "Red Scare," including raids on suspected citizens and political headquarters directed by U.S. attorney general A. Mitchell Palmer. Numerous Americans, including the prominent and courageous labor leader and presidential candidate Eugene Debs, were imprisoned for their "subversive" ideas—not one of the finer chapters in the history of freedom in America.

Until roughly the coming of the New Deal of Franklin Roosevelt in 1933, workingmen and -women who struck for higher wages, better working conditions, or simply for the recognition by their employers of their labor union were frequently attacked and terrorized by hired thugs and strikebreakers. My doctoral dissertation told the story of such brutal tactics used by the coal barons against their miners in the Colorado coal strike of 1913–14, which ended in the "Ludlow Massacre" of April 1914. A dozen women and children encamped in tents near Ludlow, Colorado, were suffocated when strikebreakers and units of the Colorado National Guard burned the tents in a pitched battle with the striking miners. After unrest spread throughout the southern Colorado coal fields, President Woodrow Wilson sent in a large contingent of federal troops to quell the violence and the strike soon ended.

An even more serious and far-reaching "Red Scare" developed after World War II, orchestrated by such political demagogues as Wisconsin senator Joe McCarthy and California congressman Richard Nixon, which tainted American politics and society in the late 1940s and 1950s. Democratic senator Pat McCarran of Nevada provided a bipartisan flavor to the fear-peddling. These fear peddlers contended that America was being undermined by Communists and their sympathizers across the country and in all of our institutions. Even Hollywood actors, actresses, producers, and writers were blacklisted for alleged Communist leanings. Some of our most loquacious politicians professed to see communism sweeping the world. Democrats strove mightily to match the anti-Communist rhetoric of the more hard-line Republicans, but they could never quite duplicate the militant anti-Communist oratory of McCarthyism.

Despite such scare tactics, President Eisenhower knew where to look for padding and waste in the Pentagon budget. He had the self-confidence to say no to costly new weapons systems that he believed added little or nothing to our security. Beyond this, as an old-fashioned conservative, Ike did not want the federal government to sink further into debt for weapons beyond the needs of a well-rounded national defense.

The aging, experienced general also understood that if the Pentagon claims too much of the federal budget, it deprives us of other sources of national strength—education, child nutrition, health care, transportation, and a balanced federal budget. Defense is important, but it cannot be secured simply by bigger and more numerous weapons.

I beg my readers to read and ponder the following paragraphs copied from President Eisenhower's memoirs after he completed his eight years in the White House:

> During the years of my Presidency, and especially the latter years, I began to feel more and more uneasiness about the effect on the nation of tremendous peacetime military expenditures. . . .
>
> With victory in World War II we began to reduce our forces so precipitously that every year from 1947 to 1950—on the eve of the Korean War—our annual military budget never exceeded $12 billion.
>
> But in mid-1953, after the end of the Korean War, I determined that we would not again become so weak militarily as to encourage aggression. This decision demanded a military budget that would establish, by its very size, a peacetime precedent. . . .
>
> The effects of these expenditures on the nation's economy would be serious. Some of these effects would surely be seen as beneficial. But their eventual influence on our national life, unless watched by an alert citizenry, could become almost overpowering.
>
> To counter this caution, there are, of course, other interested parties. Many groups find much value to themselves in constant increases in defense expenditures. The military services, traditionally concerned

with 100 per cent security, are rarely satisfied with the amounts allocated to them, out of an even generous budget.

The makers of the expensive munitions of war, to be sure, like the profits they receive, and the greater the expenditures the more lucrative the profits. Under the spur of profit potential, powerful lobbies spring up to argue for even larger munitions expenditures. And the web of special interest grows.

Each community in which a manufacturing plant or a military installation is located profits from the money spent and the jobs created in the area. This fact, of course, constantly presses on the community's political representatives—congressmen, senators, and others—to maintain the facility at maximum strength.

All of these forces, and more, tend, therefore, to override the convictions of responsible officials who are determined to have a defense structure of adequate size but are equally determined that it shall not grow beyond that level. In the long run, the combinations of pressures for growth can create an almost overpowering influence. Unjustified military spending is nothing more than a distorted use of the nation's resources.

In the making of every military budget, my associates and I were guided by these considerations. We did our best to achieve real security without surrendering to special interest.

The idea, then, of making a final address as President to the nation seemed to call on me to warn the nation, again, of the danger in these developments. I could think of no better way to emphasize this than to include a sobering message in what might otherwise have been a farewell of pleasantries.

The most quoted section of the speech came in these paragraphs:

"A vital element in keeping the peace is our military establishment. Our arms must be mighty, ready for instant action, so that no potential aggressor may be tempted to risk his own destruction.

"Our military organization today bears little relation to that known by any of my predecessors in peacetime, or indeed by the fighting men of World War II or Korea.

"Until the latest of our world conflicts, the United States had no armaments industry. American makers of plowshares could, with time and as required, make swords as well. But now we can no longer risk emergency improvisation of national defense; we have been compelled to create a permanent armaments industry of vast proportions. Added to this, three and a half million men and women are directly engaged in the defense establishment. We annually spend on military security more than the net income of all United States corporations.

"This conjunction of an immense military establishment and a large arms industry is new in the American experience. The total influence—economic, political, even spiritual—is felt in every city, every state house, every office of the federal government. We recognize the imperative need for this development. Yet we must not fail to comprehend its grave implications. Our toil, resources, and livelihood are all involved; so is the very structure of our society.

"In the councils of government we must guard against the acquisition of unwarranted influence, whether sought or unsought, by the military-industrial complex. The potential for the disastrous rise of misplaced power exists and will persist.

"We must never let the weight of this combination endanger our liberties or democratic processes. We should take nothing for granted. Only an alert and knowledgeable citizenry can compel the proper meshing of the huge industrial and military machinery of defense with our peaceful methods and goals, so that security and liberty may prosper together."

This was, at the end of my years in the White House, the most challenging message I could leave with the people of this country.

The next morning I held my final news conference. In the last question a reporter asked: ". . . would you sum up for us your idea of what kind of a United States you would like your grandchildren to live in?" My answer summed up all I'd been trying to do for eight years:

I hoped that they might live "in a peaceful world . . . enjoying all of the privileges and carrying forward all the responsibilities envisioned for the good citizen of the United States, and this means among other things the effort always to raise the standards of our people in their spiritual . . . intellectual . . . [and] economic strength. That's what I would like to see them have." (*Waging Peace*, pp. 614–17)

Recognizing that we cannot anticipate all potential threats to our nation and its interests, I suggest that we carefully reduce military spending in stages over the next ten years.

The president should propose to the Joint Chiefs of Staff, the Office of Management and Budget (OMB), and the appropriate congressional committees a military budget cut of $25 billion for next year and for each subsequent year until we reach an annual outlay of $250 billion for military purposes in the tenth year. These annual cuts would require vigorous, disciplined judgments by our top military officers, OMB, and the Congress. But I firmly believe that we have the qualities of imagination, innovation, and common sense in the men and women of the armed services, in our budget office, and in the Congress who, working together, could keep our country well defended at half the current cost if we gave them a decade to accomplish the task.

In an excellent lead editorial of February 4, 2004, *The New York Times* illustrated how hundreds of billions of dollars could be saved over the next twenty years in the Pentagon's proposed weapons spending.

"What begs for drastic surgery are the expensive weapons programs predicated on the unlikely notion of a conflict between two technologically advanced superpowers. Cutting these unneeded programs might weaken the profit outlook for defense contractors like Lockheed Martin, Boeing, Northrop Grumman and Raytheon. It would not weaken the war on terrorism," wrote the *Times* editor.

The Pentagon is now pushing for three advanced-tactical and Joint Strike fighter airplanes: the F-22 of the Air Force, the Navy's F-18, and a third plane, the E-35, to be shared by the two services. The weakness of this scheme, costing several hundreds of billions of dollars over the next twenty years, is not that the airplanes are duds. They are all state-of-the-art aircraft. But so are the airplanes they will be replacing, which are clearly superior to the planes of any other country and to anything any country can launch for many years to come.

Here is a huge military outlay of the kind approved year after year when our defense planners thought it necessary for us to be ready for a war to the death against the Soviet Union and China simultaneously.

As an old bomber pilot, I have a small bias on the side of the Air Force. But how can we refute the findings of the *Times* editor: "Harder to justify is increasing Air Force spending by 9.6 percent while holding the Army to a 1.8 percent increase. The Army has borne the brunt of recent fighting and is still stretched to the breaking point"?

After pointing up the unreliability of the Star Wars missile defense scheme, the *Times* sees another $10 billion to be saved here by delaying any deployment of the system until research has demonstrated its worth.

"The strong defense everybody wants will not come

from throwing ever larger sums into the wrong weapons. It can come only from spending responsible amounts on the right priorities," concludes the *Times*.

And to that I say, Amen.

Needless to say, if conditions in the world should change and our military leaders and the Congress decided that we should postpone an annual cut—perhaps even increase military spending—we could make such an adjustment.

Chapter 3

LIBERALISM AND CONSERVATISM:

THE AMERICAN CONDITION AND HOW WE GOT HERE

The spirit of liberty is the spirit that is not too sure it is right.

—JUDGE LEARNED HAND

THE MOST PRACTICAL and hopeful compass to guide the American ship of state is the philosophy of liberalism. Always under attack from those who want the government to do little except cut taxes for the wealthy and increase federal spending for the Pentagon and its corporate allies, liberalism's role is to harness federal power to serve the public interest. I challenge my conservative friends to name a single federal program now generally approved by both of our major parties that was not first pushed by liberals over the opposition of conservatives.

Consider Medicare, which no politician would even think of opposing today. When it was first advanced by liberals, conservatives cried "socialism." Indeed, my friend George Bush Sr.—then a congressman—predicted that if Congress adopted Medicare, the American health care system would collapse. I'm pleased that our former president long ago changed his mind. Changing one's mind is not a sin. Indeed, it is a way of saying that I'm wiser today than I was yesterday. (The senior George Bush has my esteem for his courageous war record as a young man and for his lifetime of public service.)

Social Security—an FDR liberal proposal—frightened conservatives into their closets. But today is there a politician of either major party who will stand up and attack Social Security? Even Ronald Reagan, who detested most U.S. government programs except for the military, a part of the government he never experienced except in movies, finally embraced Social Security. He was wiser than he was the day before.

The free market is often cited by conservatives as a more dependable institution than the federal government. But as we learned in the crash of our economy in 1929, and more recently in the shocking behavior of some of our largest corporations, there is such a thing as an economy that is too free. I concluded many years ago that our economy serves us best when it is humanized by appropriate public regulations and laws that are enforced by dedicated public servants.

In recent times, no nation has built a more prosperous,

productive economy than the United States. No American president has presided over a stronger stock market, with improvements in employment, productivity, interest rates, and business earnings, than President Clinton with the invaluable counsel of his great secretary of the Treasury, Robert Rubin. But over the past three years of the Bush administration, the stock market has been erratic, unemployment is too high, and the annual federal deficit is again zooming upward after being in surplus in the year 2000.

Beyond this, the economy and the American people are now suffering from President Bush's ill-advised, huge tax giveaway to the wealthiest individuals and corporations while simultaneously escalating military spending—a formula for a once again rising national debt. Business failures are increasing, and, most embarrassing of all, some of our major corporations—Enron, WorldCom, Tyco, Arthur Andersen, and others—have been engaged in shockingly corrupt practices. Enron's executives, for example, manipulated their books and enriched themselves while exploiting their workers, pensioners, and stockholders. Some used their inside knowledge to unload their soon-to-collapse stock and fill their own coffers with untold millions of dollars while concealing the rotten core of their corporation from those who trusted them. The massive corruption of Enron makes Martha Stewart's minor mischief seem like relatively insignificant wrongdoing.

What was missing with Enron and other giant corporations was not a strong economy, but a moral sense of decency and honesty on the part of executives who sank their corporations in a sea of double-dealing and greed. The remedy? Plain old-fashioned morality and common sense, as embodied in our founding documents and the faith of our fathers.

Our current president wants to invest the Social Security Trust Fund in the stock market; but with the market going soft and wobbly, and large corporations collapsing from mismanagement and dishonest accounting practices, is that a safe depository for the public's trust fund?

Who really wants to put the Social Security Trust Fund in the hands of Enron, WorldCom, and other once respected corporations, with Arthur Andersen cooking the books? The free market may sound like a good slogan, but not when it means freedom for unethical corporate raiders to rob their stockholders, their employees, their worker pension funds, and the American public. And it is no answer that independent fund managers can protect our investments. Even while Enron executives were selling their shares for countless millions, the New York City pension program lost $109 million on Enron shares it had purchased. Florida's pension fund lost $335 million in the Enron heist. A total of 571 mutual funds that had purchased Enron stock while Enron's corporate executives were dumping theirs lost many millions of dollars.

If the country's mutual fund managers lost their shirts with Enron, why would these great stock investors do any better playing off our Social Security Trust Fund in the stock market, as now recommended by the Bush administration?

In addition to the liberal innovations mentioned above,

there are a host of others that have enriched our lives, including guaranteed bank deposits, the Securities and Exchange Commission, the Federal Reserve, the Food and Drug Administration, the National Park Service, the Forest Service, the Federal School Lunch Program, Food Stamps for low-income families, the WIC program, which provides nutritional supplements for low-income pregnant and nursing mothers and their infants through the age of five, the Voting Rights Act, Equal Access to Public Accommodations, Collective Bargaining and Fair Labor Standards, the graduated income tax, the Clean Air Act, the Clean Water Act, equal rights for women, and earned income tax credits for workers. Every one of these efforts, which strengthened our democracy and the quality of life in America, began as a liberal initiative contested by conservatives.

One of the truly historic achievements of liberalism was the civil rights revolution of the 1950s and 1960s, which at long last redeemed the promise of Jefferson's Declaration that "all men [and women] are created equal."

I have no enmity toward conservatives. A treasured political ally and friend is Senator Bob Dole—a true "compassionate conservative" and one of our national treasures. And consider my dear parents—lifetime conservatives. They would have regarded my friendship with Bob Dole as the crowning achievement of my political life! They would also have been pleased with my longtime friendship with Barry Goldwater and with Republican senators Mark Hatfield, George Aiken, Jacob Javits, John Sherman Cooper, John Chafee, Jim Pearson, Al Simpson, and Dick Lugar. But many conservatives see their role as blocking anything the government attempts on behalf of the ordinary American. In foreign policy they tend to be isolationists, opposed to the United Nations, and against international assistance— except possibly selling or giving military hardware to selected despots.

I want to be fair about this. I have suggested that there is no federal program now generally approved by both liberals and conservatives that did not begin as a liberal initiative over conservative opposition. The other side of this equation is that I can think of no federal initiative now endorsed by liberals and conservatives alike that began as a conservative initiative over liberal opposition. If there is such an example hidden away in the political woodwork, I trust some reader will point it out to me.

Some readers may assume that my vigorous liberalism is influenced in part by my overwhelming defeat by President Richard Nixon, who was forced to leave office in disgrace after the election because of the Watergate scandal. But I bear no malice toward Mr. Nixon. Indeed, he governed as a moderate liberal. His administration launched the Environmental Protection Agency, he supported civil rights, he established détente with the Soviet Union and opened the door to China, he invoked wage and price controls to stabilize the economy—just to name a few of his moderately liberal steps. What promised to be an even more promising second term was ended in the revealed cover-up of wrongdoing during his campaign against me. But just to keep matters in perspective, I regard Mr. Nixon as a far wiser president than the present occupant of the White House. I would say the same about the senior President Bush—

another moderate liberal with a brilliant combat record in World War II.

Since this book attempts to construct a design for a greater America in a more peaceful world, I want to lay my cards on the table now so readers will know where I'm going, possibly giving some the opportunity to bail out. Here is how I see it. There is not much of a future for America in today's conservatism. It has become narrow, negative, and doctrinaire, made less acceptable by its current far-to-the-right extremism. It keeps the train rusting away on the tracks but can't move it out of the station and on its way to Peoria and Chattanooga.

We need the conservatives to challenge liberal ideas and impel us to examine their soundness. But we can't expect today's conservatives to offer positive ideas of their own. Conservatives may cling stubbornly to their views, which in one sense is admirable, but positive and creative?—no way. Nothing inspiring has come out of the conservative mind since the age of John Adams. This is assuming that Lincoln, the first Republican president, and Theodore Roosevelt, who opened up the twentieth century, were liberals, which they certainly were—more so than many Democrats, as were such Republican senators as George Norris of Nebraska, Bob La Follette of Wisconsin, and Peter Norbeck of South Dakota.

America has always needed the vitality and redeeming strength of the liberal spirit sharpened by the anvil of conservatism. Some of our hesitant and ambivalent colonial forebears needed to hear the call to freedom and independence of Tom Paine's *Common Sense* and the pure liberalism of Jefferson's Declaration of Independence. When the future of the Union hung in the balance, the nation desperately needed the compassionate and liberal-minded Lincoln at the helm. Lincoln was always more liberal than many of the Whigs and Democrats of his day. That's why he helped found a new political party—the Republican Party. Lincoln's liberalism also went beyond the leanings of many of today's alleged liberals. He believed, for example, that laboring people were the backbone of the economy—more important than the capitalists at the top.

At the dawning of the twentieth century, America moved forward with the New Nationalism of Theodore Roosevelt, the New Freedom of Woodrow Wilson, and the New Deal of Franklin Roosevelt—three liberal presidents. Three subsequent presidents who advanced the liberal agenda were Harry Truman, John Kennedy, and Lyndon Johnson. Two southern governors who became Democratic presidents—Jimmy Carter and Bill Clinton—also advanced some liberal ideas, but they might not want me to call them liberals—although they are compassionate, liberal-minded men of broad vision.

Of late, we have heard much about the trials and tribulations of liberalism. It does seem to be increasingly difficult for liberals to get elected and equally difficult to advance a liberal agenda if they are elected. Indeed, some contemporary liberals would just as soon keep their liberalism a secret. "I'm neither liberal nor conservative. I'm a pragmatic progressive," I heard one prominent liberal assert on television recently. Apparently, "pragmatic progressive" is safer than the "L" word. Staying with PP, another liberal has described himself as a progressive pragmatist. I'm not quite certain of the ideological difference between a "pragmatic progressive" and a "progressive pragmatist," but it must be profound. We can only hope that PP doesn't conjure up childhood references to what we told Mama we needed to do when nature came calling.

Professor H. W. Brands of Texas A&M, who has given us two excellent biographies of two great liberals, Theodore Roosevelt and Benjamin Franklin, has now put forth a challenging new book, *The Strange Death of American Liberalism*. As an admirer of Professor Brands, I must say that I disagree almost entirely with both the title and the central thesis of this latest book. To start with, liberalism is not dead. Indeed, I fully expect liberalism to be stronger and more successful over the next twenty-five years than during the past twenty-five. I say that because most of our problems can be solved only by liberal solutions—as has been true historically.

Most of today's liberals are too intimidated and cautious for my taste. But liberalism has been a continuous political force in America for two hundred years and will certainly survive as long as its competing tradition—conservatism. Just about every educated person I encounter around the world is a liberal. Just about every working journalist I meet is a liberal, although not the publisher-owners. Just about every nurse, airline flight attendant, teacher, professor, organized worker, scientist, foreign service officer, writer, poet, artist, actor, actress, singer, musician, clergyman, environmentalist, child care worker, and waiter—nearly all of these are liberals. Most women seem to be liberals, as are Indians, blacks, Hispanics, and other minorities. I seldom meet an illiberal professor of history—my old profession. I found it difficult to read history and retain the conservatism of my youth, but of course some have been able to accomplish that feat.

It is my own view that the Cold War has been the most destructive enemy of liberalism over the last half century. This was especially true during the endless and hopeless Vietnam War—the biggest albatross of the Cold War. That massive mistake in American foreign policy tore American liberalism asunder and divided it into "hawks" and "doves." I never liked either of those labels, but the division was real. There can be no doubt that President Lyndon Johnson went to his grave grieving over the obvious fact that his dream of a Great Society in America was partly lost in the jungles of Indochina. Senators and congressmen who served during the endless Cold War, with its huge demands on the federal budget, understood that the fiscal burden, inflationary pressure, and wartime tax levels made it politically difficult and hazardous to add on still more funds for liberal domestic programs.

Conservatives with a reactionary streak discredited liberals by suggesting that they were bordering the camp of the Socialists and Communists. It was not nearly so effective for liberals to suggest that conservatives sometimes climbed into bed with Fascists. The conservatives even charged that Communists had infiltrated American liberalism, or that at the least, liberals were soft on communism. This, of course, was a lie, but an effective lie. David P. Barash deals effectively with this phenomenon in his brilliant, powerful book *The L Word.* With huge campaign war chests, clever political propagandists, and a mighty army of radio and later TV right-wing talk show hosts, conservative candidates depicted their liberal opponents as weak on national defense, indifferent to family values, soft on communism, and captives of the welfare lobby, the gun controllers, and the abortionists. This is the false and destructive propaganda that defeated many a Democratic liberal, including a massacre of key liberal senators in 1980—Frank Church, Gaylord Nelson, Birch Bayh, John Culver, and yours truly. We were targeted for political defeat by a coalition of reactionary right-wing groups adept at the politics of slander. The U.S. Senate has never fully recovered from this 1980 extremist massacre. This was also the year when President Jimmy Carter, a decent, hardworking, dedicated president, was defeated by Ronald Reagan. The first Sunday after the 1980 election, one of Reagan's biggest financial backers was quoted: "We not only elected Ronnie; we got rid of that son-of-a-bitch in South Dakota."

Professor Arthur Schlesinger Jr. has argued for years that there is a rhythm in the cycles of liberalism and conservatism—that the two central traditions of our history take turns dominating our politics. Liberalism is in the saddle for a while with a more activist federal government devoted to rank-and-file Americans. People eventually tire of this and move to conservatism, with its more quiescent government, less regulation, and the promise of lower taxes. Then various groups, including many women, minorities, workers, environmentalists, teachers, farmers, and peace advocates, begin to agitate, and conservatism gives way to another liberal cycle.

I find this analysis more compelling than Professor Brands's. Liberals have been out of power most of the time since 1969, and they are about due for another ride—if they will just shed a little of their timidity and come out swinging, as recommended by the inimitable James Carville and as demonstrated by former Vermont governor Howard Dean, the man who defined the Democratic presidential race of 2004. Dean did not win the nomination, but he demonstrated how Democrats could defeat President Bush. He also brought a huge army of first-time voters into Democratic ranks. I believe that President Bush will likely be a one-term president—partly because of Howard Dean.

A political leader has the obligation to try to understand the public will, but not necessarily to be controlled by it. He must also identify as best he can the mistaken aspects of the public will and of government policy. He should seek to lay bare the malfunctions of our body politic so that sensible repairs can be prescribed. Beyond this, a political leader should offer a vision that can light the way to the days and years ahead.

Shortly after I had won the Democratic presidential nomination in 1972, my friend and longtime colleague Senator Fritz Hollings of South Carolina stopped me on the floor of the Senate and said: "Well, George, I don't claim to have voted for you to be our presidential nominee, and I doubt that you or any other Democrat can upset Nixon, but you have the best sense of the country's greatness of all the candidates running this year." That, to me, was the highest and most meaningful compliment I received on the 1972 effort. Senator Hollings's words represented what I most wanted to achieve in seeking the highest office in the land—to call the nation home to the ideals of the founders: Jefferson's "Life, Liberty and the pursuit of Happiness" and "a decent respect to the opinions of mankind" and Lincoln's "government of the people, by the people, for the people"—a government that would appeal "to the better angels of our nature."

Second only to the words of Senator Hollings, I treasured the comment in 1972 of the chairman of the History Department of the University of South Dakota, the late Professor Herbert Schell. When asked by an out-of-state reporter what, if anything, was unique about me as a presidential nominee, Dr. Schell replied: "He is the only nominee of either major party since World War II who has not accepted the assumptions of the Cold War." I never knew whether Professor Schell was a Democrat or a Republican. He guarded his reputation for objectivity in the classroom carefully. But I always liked what he told that reporter.

As a straightforward patriot and a strong advocate of constitutional democracy, I trust that my campaigns for the House and Senate and for the presidency, including criticism of certain policies and priorities, were a manifestation of my faith in the American heritage. Patriotism includes the responsibility when the nation is following an unwise course to call it to a higher standard. To the self-styled patriot with his bumper sticker "America, Love It or Leave It," I would respond, "America, let us improve it so we may love it the more." Or, if you prefer the words of Carl Schurz: "Our country, right or wrong! When right, may we uphold the right. When wrong, may we correct the wrong. But our country, right or wrong!"

I believe in the essential decency and fairness of the American people. That doesn't mean, however, that either our leaders or the voters are always of sound judgment. Freedom of choice includes the right to be wrong as well as to be right. Democracy does not guarantee wisdom or virtue; it offers freedom and majority rule. We can only hope that the majority and our leaders will be right from time to time.

After a lifetime of studying political systems, the late distinguished Williams College professor Frederick L. Schuman concluded: "Electorates are fickle, skeptical, indifferent, ignorant and perverse." (*International Politics,* 1948, p. 391)

Perhaps this is the two-way gamble of democracy. The voters gamble when they give their votes to a candidate for high office. The candidate gambles when he submits himself to the judgment of the voters. Despite the hazard of free choice, I still prefer it to the dictates of tyranny. But anyone who aspires to high office should fortify himself with the knowledge that the public and the press are no more certain of what is best for the nation than are the politicians. We are all functioning with uncertainties and limited knowledge. And we all, at times, behave in foolish and irrational ways.

The incredibly mistaken American war in Vietnam is perhaps the most glaring recent illustration of an irrational policy advocated by both of our major political parties, most of the Congress, most of the press, and most of the American public.

Our leaders should have listened to the words of General Douglas MacArthur, who said after the Korean War in testimony to the Senate Armed Services Committee in 1953: "Any Commander-in-Chief who ever again commits American troops to the Asian mainland ought to have his head examined."

This thirty years' war in Vietnam, 1945–75, waged by the French and then by Americans against Vietnamese independence, was an outgrowth of an even larger policy mistake—our greatly exaggerated notion of the Soviet threat. It was prudent for us to keep abreast of Soviet military capabilities and international objectives. But it always seemed to me that the enormous and frightfully costly nuclear arsenal that we built up, supposedly to keep the Soviets from overrunning Europe or engaging in mutual suicide with a nuclear attack on the United States, was extravagantly overdone. We could have cut the military budget in half at any time in the last fifty years and been a stronger and more secure nation in doing so. The same thing goes for the $30 billion annual budget of the Central Intelligence Agency and the other spy agencies. And the same went for the Soviet military and the KGB. The Soviet Union, an economically poor country compared to the United States, might still be intact if it had not broken the bank trying to match the enormous U.S. military colossus.

In a real sense, the excessive military outlays of Washington and Moscow weakened both countries, finally breaking the Soviet system and its state-controlled economy. The United States, with its greater wealth and power and its democratic political system, survived the half century of Cold War, but at a heavy price. We consistently ran large deficits with a huge national debt at the expense of our taxpayers. Similarly, escalating arms spending deprived us of resources needed to upgrade our central cities, rebuild our decaying infrastructure, develop alternative sources of energy, construct a modern railway and public transit system, protect our environment and stop global warming, strengthen our education, and provide needed health care. Beyond this, by concentrating three fourths of our scientific and technical research and development on the arms industry, we deprived our civilian industry of needed improvements. In automobiles, for example, we lost our clear number one position to Japan. Other countries surpassed us in railways and trains, steel and electronics. Perhaps most costly of all is that we resorted to a whole range of sordid tactics to win the Cold War that weakened our moral and political standing around the world. The term "superpower" described our nuclear arsenal, not the measure of our moral might, which was steadily degraded during the Cold War.

By constantly escalating the arms race, the Cold War came to dominate American foreign policy and to control the priorities of the nation at home and abroad. It was only by accepting these Cold War assumptions that our entry into Vietnam made any sense. If the Soviets controlled a monolithic global Communist apparatus and this was the

72

central threat to America, then why not take on the Communists wherever they appeared, including Vietnam or even tiny Cuba?

It was this Cold War assumption that the USSR was the overarching threat to America that led us to embrace even the most corrupt Fascist dictators as long as they waved an anti-Soviet banner. That is why we entered the Vietnam fray in 1945 by backing the failing French effort to regain their colonial hold over Indochina. We did this to win French support against the Russians in Europe. Never mind that this action was a betrayal of our historic commitment to the self-determination of nations.

A related paradox has always intrigued me: Why did we eventually come to recognize and trade with the big Communist nations, the USSR and China, while boycotting the little Communist states? Cuba especially comes to mind. We have carried on normal diplomatic and trading relations with Russia since 1933 and with China since 1972. But impoverished little Cuba, with its 9 million people, we regard as too threatening to recognize. Some say that this is because Cuba is only ninety miles from Miami. But Russian submarines that could have obliterated our largest cities cruised a few hundred miles off our shores for years—far closer and more dangerous than Cuba. No, there is something else behind our boycott of Cuba other than national security. Could it be simply old-fashioned nonsense or a case of down-home paranoia? Or has the world's greatest superpower been willing to let the noisiest Cuban exiles in Miami dictate our Cuban policy for forty years?

In trying to understand our thirty-year intervention

in Vietnam, the quarter-of-a-century refusal to recognize China, and the forty-year policy of boycotting Cuba, it is helpful to recall editor John Fisher's decades-old article in *Harper's* magazine entitled "The Stupidity Factor." As with our failed policy in Vietnam, where we eventually stood alone in the world, no other country on the planet supports our Cuban policy. Again, we are all alone, and again, we are plainly wrong. Just as an irrational policy in Vietnam weakened our position in the eyes of the world, so are we weakened by a foolish, self-defeating policy toward Cuba.

The reader has doubtless concluded by now that in politics and international affairs, I am a confirmed and proud liberal with a certain respect for honest-to-goodness conservatives. I admire conservatives who sincerely say what they think. My favorite conservatives, such as the deceased Barry Goldwater, Bob Dole, Al Simpson of Wyoming, and columnist Bill Buckley, also have a sense of humor. There is no surplus of humor and wit in American politics. Loyal liberal that I am, I would rather go fishing with a conservative endowed by a humorous streak than with a humorless liberal.

Liberalism is the most maligned political philosophy in contemporary history. The negative associations of the word are now so pronounced that some political campaigners assert that the opponent has been practicing "liberalism"— as though this were sufficient to consign the "guilty" liberal to ridicule and defeat.

It is all the more notable that even many liberals have lapsed into a reluctance to defend the liberal record. As the poet Robert Frost once observed: "A liberal is someone who won't take his own side in a quarrel."

Is it possible that liberalism—one of America's central political traditions from the beginning—has betrayed its proud heritage? Or have recent generations evaluated the liberal record accurately and found it unacceptable? Or have political enemies of liberalism so unfairly maligned it that large numbers of people equate the manufactured distortion with liberalism itself? Or is Professor Brands, who has performed an autopsy on the liberal body and found that it died with the death of the Cold War, right in his view? Or have all of these factors combined to leave the self-confessed liberal a victim of confusion and contempt?

I believe that most Americans are either liberals or, at the least, have some liberal impulses. There are, of course, those among us who are prepared to condemn without reservation liberalism and all of its works. But few of them seem to grasp the actual record of liberalism as a leavening and enriching influence in our society.

I regret that in today's politics the conservative tradition has been pushed so far to the right that it presents itself as extremism rather than authentic conservatism. Is it conservative for a president to cut his tax revenues while waging a costly, ill-advised war that has thrown the federal budget into huge deficits and a skyrocketing national debt that our children and grandchildren will have to pay in the form of heavy interest charges for many years? Is it conservatism for an administration to draft a national energy policy behind the closed door of the vice president's office and then refuse a request by Congress to know who the industrialists were who drafted an energy policy that will affect all of us?

Is it conservatism for the administration to push through

the misnamed Patriot Act, which jeopardizes the Bill of Rights?

Is it conservatism for the administration and some members of Congress to embrace the "religious Right," which is neither "religious" nor "right" but a collection of right-wing ideologues far from the American mainstream with a jaded view of our constitutional democracy?

Is it conservatism for the Bush team to ask the U.S. Supreme Court to set aside the Florida Supreme Court's ruling and in a 5 to 4 decision halt the recount in Florida in the presidential race of 2000? One would think that a true conservative would recognize that the Florida court should have had jurisdiction over these matters involving the conduct of an election in Florida.

Is it conservatism for an administration to play fast and loose with the conservation of the nation's wildlife refuges, its clean air and water, and its physical environment?

Is it conservatism to permit millions of workers to go without jobs? What can be a greater loss to our economy and our society than to idle millions of our workforce?

Liberals need to look critically at their battered tradition, but conservatives need to look critically at their tradition and bring it back from its flirtation with extremism. The genius of the American political system is the creative tension and competition between liberalism and conservatism. When either of these traditions is maligned or weakened, we all suffer. So, long live conservatism. Long live liberalism.

Chapter 4

THE CHANGING CHARACTER OF THE LIBERAL- CONSERVATIVE EQUATION

I hold it that a little rebellion now and then is a good thing, and as necessary in the political world as storms in the physical.

—THOMAS JEFFERSON, IN A LETTER TO
JAMES MADISON, JANUARY 1787

PERHAPS AT THIS POINT we need to establish an acceptable definition of "liberalism." *Webster's Dictionary* may not be the last word, but it may be an okay place to begin: "a political philosophy based on belief in progress, the essential goodness of man, and the autonomy of the individual and standing for the protection of political and civil liberties." With reference to "the essential goodness of man," the theologian Reinhold Niebuhr would modify this thought by observing: "Man's capacity for justice makes democracy possible, but man's inclination to injustice makes democracy necessary."

One assumes that liberalism would be acceptable to most Americans. It is difficult—especially in America—to ignore "belief in progress." From the beginning, Americans have believed that their conditions of life could and would be improved. This, of course, requires change in public policy from time to time as conditions change. That belief motivated much of the early and continuing migration to America. It fueled the westward flow of the advancing American frontier, which one of our greatest historians—Frederick Jackson Turner—concluded was a key to America's democratic development, at least until 1890.

As for belief in "the essential goodness of man," one cannot conceive of a nation dedicated to democracy, with its principles of majority rule, that does not at least believe its citizens have the capacity for goodness. My conservative sometime debate opponent William F. Buckley has observed, "From time to time it is . . . appropriate to wonder about the judgment of the majority." As a presidential contender who in 1972 lost forty-nine states to Richard Nixon eighteen months before he resigned the presidency in disgrace, I confess to sharing occasionally Mr. Buckley's wonderment about the majority! My wife, Eleanor, who doubtless has an elevated view of my virtues, is still baffled, especially that the South Dakota majority thought they would be better off with Nixon in the White House than with their own native son.

It is, nonetheless, doubtful that democracy could have arisen, save for a general belief in the goodness and common sense of the citizenry—a faith that has guided my own political career. It would seem even more likely in a democratic society that most of the citizenry would accept the importance of "the autonomy of the individual"—personal freedom—combined with "the protection of political and civil liberties."

But the case for and against liberalism is not captured entirely by the dictionary definition. Liberalism since the days of Thomas Jefferson has evolved in historical stages. The most devoted liberals in today's American body politic—while paying homage to Jefferson—would be quick to recognize that just as the conditions of life and governance have changed since Jefferson's time, so has the definition and breadth of liberalism.

Jefferson believed passionately in the freedom and dignity of the individual. Fearing the reach of a centralized, interventionist national government, he preferred to see the powers of government restricted to a minimum. Such government as was necessary should be assigned mostly to state and local entities. Memories of the abuse of power by King George III doubtless made Jefferson skeptical of centralized authority. He believed in a largely unregulated, laissez-faire economy with minimum government involvement in economic affairs.

It seems clear that Jefferson's fear of central government power grew out of his ardor against the authoritarian meddling of the British crown in the affairs of the American colonies. In the Declaration, Jefferson poured forth his indignation over the abuses of George III and his colonial governors. Similarly, Jefferson feared the capacity for centralized domination in the early drafts of the U.S. Constitution. He refused even to endorse the Constitution until a Bill of Rights was added, protecting the personal freedoms of American citizens.

Jefferson's heart beat especially for the farmers, mechanics, small merchants, and laboring people of society. He saw America as an essentially rural collection of states without large cities or concentrations of economic and financial power. "The small landholder is the most precious part of the state," he contended. Cities, on the other hand, were "sores on the body politic."

Hamilton, his conservative counterpart, had a sharply different view. To him, America's destiny lay with aggressive commercial and industrial entrepreneurs aided by a strong national bank and a vigorous national government able and willing to carry a substantial national debt. It was obviously necessary to have farmers and laborers, as well as local and state governments, but these were secondary factors in the Hamiltonian scheme. His passion called for a working alliance between a strong federal government and the most powerful and privileged commercial and financial entrepreneurs.

Liberals and conservatives today can marvel at the competing positions taken by their respective patron saints relative to the role of the national government. Today's conservatives would be repelled by Hamilton's call for a more interventionist, centralizing governing authority unless such intervention were limited to advancing business interests and the military. Liberals today would find unrealistic

Jefferson's view of a severely restricted federal government with such governing power as there is concentrated in local civic bodies. In a real sense, today's liberals would be more comfortable with a vigorous, active federal government as envisioned by Hamilton but, unlike Hamilton, would direct government intervention toward the concerns of rank-and-file Americans, workers, farmers, small merchants, and the poor.

Today's conservatives would be more comfortable with the Jeffersonian model of limited federal power and laissez-faire economics—with important exceptions, including the conservative wish for federal intervention on behalf of business and corporate interests, tax privileges for higher-income citizens and corporations, and large military contracts. One substantial category of conservatives would even favor the federal government controlling such personal or family matters as abortion, the rules of marriage, and public prayer in the schools. But by and large, at least in theory, today's conservatives claim the mantle of Jefferson's early commitment to restricted federal power, whereas today's liberals call for a more actively involved federal government.

How to explain this paradox? It is the march of history and changing economic and political conditions. Political ideology does not stand still. If it were to do so, it would soon become irrelevant and die a deserved death.

Jefferson himself contended that a dynamic, democratic society should undergo revolutionary change at periodic intervals—at least every twenty years. Obviously, he would not be advocating the same political formula for today's world that he advocated for a much simpler rural community two hundred years ago.

The first significant movement of liberalism away from its Jeffersonian roots came with the administration of President Andrew Jackson—two decades after Jefferson's presidency. The Jacksonians were even more committed by social background and political inclination to the well-being of the "common man"—farmers, laborers, and small merchants—than the aristocratic Jefferson and his colleagues with their large landed estates worked by slaves.

But Jackson and his followers, having taken over the reins of government and having defeated the National Bank, began to realize that the government in their hands was not necessarily the enemy of "the humble members of society." They thus took a few cautious but historically significant steps toward a stronger federal government and one with a clearer concern for the well-being of ordinary citizens. But the Jacksonian movement did not discard Jefferson's commitment to a restricted federal government and a free, competitive economy. What concerned Jackson was not so much a laissez-faire economy, but the special privileges claimed by the rich and the powerful from a compliant government under their influence.

In his veto of the National Bank renewal bill, Jackson wrote:

> It is to be regretted that the rich and powerful too often bend the acts of government to their selfish purposes. In the full enjoyment of the gifts of Heaven and the fruits of superior industry, economy and

virtue, every man is equally entitled to protection by law; but when the laws undertake to add to these natural and just advantages artificial distinctions, to grant titles, gratuities and exclusive privileges, to make the rich richer and the potent more powerful, the humble members of society—the farmers, mechanics and laborers—who have neither the time nor the means of securing like favors to themselves, have a right to complain of the injustice of their government.

Although not directly challenging the Jeffersonian view of weak government and an unregulated free economy, Jackson and his followers took the first modest steps, as Arthur Schlesinger Jr. wrote in his classic study of the Jacksonian age, of seeking Jeffersonian ends with Hamiltonian means. In other words, a stronger, more positive government devoted not to the wealthy and powerful but to the "common people" of America.

From that day to this, liberals have resisted the power of concentrated wealth and big business in the contest for control of the government. If there is any one overall defining difference between liberalism and conservatism throughout our history, it has been the effort of liberals to utilize the powers of government to serve the well-being of rank-and-file Americans, as compared to the conservative preference for government with a special concern for maintaining the stability and prosperity of the business and commercial interests of the nation.

Liberals would argue, with some historical support, that even business and industry do better when farmers, workers, small merchants, and senior citizens flourish with the help of liberal government. But the progress of liberalism was slow and uncertain in the century following the Jacksonian era.

Through most of the nineteenth and early twentieth centuries, business interests more often than not held sway for federal favors. The building of canals and roadways, the land grants to the railroad builders, high tariffs, a favorable tax code, lack of concern for the rights and conditions of labor, a virtually free hand for banks and large corporations—these and other favors to business far outweighed any advantages secured from government by small merchants, farmers, or the elderly and the poor. The two major political parties—Democrats and Republicans—did not by and large take issue with these prevailing nineteenth-century tendencies. Even the abuses of the "robber barons" in mercilessly exploiting the nation's resources and the public trust were not seriously challenged by either of our major parties for most of the nineteenth century.

The first serious challenge to this comfortable system from those who believed that government ought to be a public instrument to combat injustice and corruption came from the Populists. This largely rural-based movement sought to protect farmers from discriminatory railroad shipping rates, excessive credit costs, and unfair banking and insurance practices. The Populists also sought a graduated income tax—later to become one of the cardinal tenets of American liberalism.

In 1896, the Populists took control of the Democratic Party by nominating William Jennings Bryan for the presidency. As Milton Viorst noted: "For the first time since the Jackson era, the major parties offered the voters clear-cut alternatives on basic economic and political questions." (*Liberalism: A Guide to the Past, Present, and Future in American Politics,* 1963, pp. 41–42)

Bryan advocated strong presidential leadership. In the historic "Cross of Gold" speech that led to his nomination, he asserted that "in this land of the free, you need not fear that a tyrant will spring up from among the people. What we need is an Andrew Jackson to stand, as Jackson stood, against the encroachments of organized wealth." As Viorst pointed out: "Bryan struck a note that is now familiar to American liberalism. It recognized that Jefferson had erred in designating government the greatest threat to the good society. It acknowledged the growth of institutions that had become far stronger than government and that could be as oppressive as the worst medieval tyrannies. To liberals, positive leadership of government has become the only answer to the studied weakness of the presidency that enabled the captains of industry to ravage society." (p. 42)

As the followers of Jackson and Bryan had come to see in their separate ways divided by six decades, government could be a powerful instrument in the hands of an awakened public serving the interests of the common citizenry.

This view was given further impetus by the Progressives in the early twentieth century. Led by Presidents Theodore Roosevelt and Woodrow Wilson and by such progressive senators as Robert La Follette of Wisconsin, George Norris of Nebraska, and Peter Norbeck and Richard Pettigrew of South Dakota, the Progressives moved liberalism into an embrace of positive federal action to resolve the nation's social, economic, and political problems. This was not the New Deal—yet to be generated in the pain of the Great Depression under the experimental tutelage of Franklin Roosevelt. But the Progressives, like the Populists before them, were laying the groundwork for Roosevelt's New Deal, Harry Truman's Square Deal, John Kennedy's New Frontier, and Lyndon Johnson's Great Society. Whereas Populist concerns had centered largely on the problems of farmers and rural America, Progressives concentrated largely on the urban problems stemming from the impact of a free-ranging industrialism, the sprawling growth of cities, and the corruption of municipal government.

Reacting to the control of government and the exploitation of the nation's resources by industrial and financial giants, the Progressives tried to put government more effectively into the hands of rank-and-file voters. They advocated direct primaries; the initiative, referendum, and recall; the direct election of U.S. senators; and women's right to vote. The Progressives challenged the methods and power of the big-city bosses and attempted to restore more competition to business by breaking up the large trusts.

They moved beyond the Jeffersonian view of restricted federal power by calling for federal regulation of the railroads and public utilities. They fought for federal laws to outlaw the exploitation of child labor, the sweatshop, and dangerous conditions in the nation's mines. The Progressives led the way in calling for the right of laboring people to organize and bargain collectively.

Progressives pushed successfully for the enactment of

a constitutional amendment authorizing the graduated income tax previously proposed by Populist reformers. They were also instrumental in the passage of the Pure Food and Drug Act, with the strong support of President Theodore Roosevelt, aided greatly by Upton Sinclair's powerful novel *The Jungle* (1900), which revealed shocking conditions and bad labor practices in the meatpacking industry. Sinclair, who was trying to spotlight the exploitation of labor in filthy meat-processing plants, said ruefully, "I reached for the head and heart of the American people, but I hit their stomachs."

Progressives also spearheaded a nationwide conservation program to protect the nation's threatened natural resources.

Led by Republican president Theodore Roosevelt and Democratic president Woodrow Wilson, the Progressives advocated liberal initiatives to achieve Jeffersonian ends, but by means of a Hamiltonian-type government.

"I stand for the square deal," Theodore Roosevelt said. "But when I say that I am for the square deal, I mean not merely that I stand for fair play under the present rules of the game, but that I stand for having those rules changed so as to work for a more substantial equality of opportunity and of reward for equally good service."

Echoing Roosevelt, Woodrow Wilson said: "We have changed our economic conditions, absolutely, from top to bottom. . . . The old political formulas do not fit the present problems. . . . A new economic society has sprung up, and we must effect a new set of adjustments."

Neither Roosevelt nor Wilson believed that the federal

government had any obligation to assist able-bodied citizens who neglected to help themselves. Neither did they believe that powerful industrial and commercial trusts should be allowed to pillage the nation's resources without restraint and use their economic and political muscle to dominate the market at the expense of small business owners, workers, and consumers. The only practical solution, they believed, was for the U.S. government to play a constructive role in advancing the interests of the American public.

Thus, in the century after Jefferson, liberals had come to the view that conditions in modern industrial America were so different from those of the simple agrarian society of Jefferson's age that two fundamental modifications needed to be made in Jeffersonian liberalism. First, a totally free market with no protection of the public was unacceptable in that it led to gigantic concentrations of economic power that would pillage and destroy the nation's natural resources while undermining smaller merchants, laborers, farmers, and the general public. In a real sense, the so-called free market tended to lead to monopoly control of the market—not to freedom. Liberals welcomed the competition of a true free economy, not the kind of monopoly power and undisciplined economic activity that in effect destroyed competition at the public's expense. Some ground rules had to be established that protected the public interest against the depredations of unrestricted business and financial greed.

Second, liberals slowly came to the conclusion that only an active, positive federal government dedicated to the well-being of the American people could correct the abuses stemming from laissez-faire economics.

Meanwhile, just as liberals were learning that a stronger, more active government in their hands could best advance the public's well-being, conservatives came to understand that such government was not compatible with their immediate desire to maximize profits and individual freedom without restraint. Many less venturesome liberals were also nervous about the extension of federal power into their lives.

As the strongest and best-organized element in the economy, the bigger industrial and commercial organizations came to believe that they were better off embracing the old Jeffersonian view—as little government as possible. If the government could no longer be counted on to be Hamiltonian in its ends—advancing the power and profits of business—then why not reduce its scope to the earlier Jeffersonian model, conservatives reasoned. If we can't any longer control government, let us at least diminish its power, they argued.

With Woodrow Wilson's absorption in the conduct of World War I, his passion for the League of Nations, and then a paralyzing stroke, his administration was not fully capable of checking the power of big business. Following Wilson, the decade of the 1920s was dominated by three conservative Republican presidents backed by business interests who believed with President Calvin Coolidge that "the business of America is business."

When the unchecked business and stock market boom collapsed in 1929, the American people lost faith in weak political leadership from Washington combined with a business-dominated laissez-faire economy. Not knowing with any certainty what the alternative political governance and economic order might be, a large majority of Americans turned to Franklin Roosevelt in the presidential election of 1932.

Roosevelt, the son of a conservative, aristocratic Hudson Valley New York family, had become a Wilson Democrat and assistant secretary of the Navy in World War I and was serving as the governor of New York when nominated for the presidency by the Democrats in 1932. He was plainly uncertain about how to proceed in dealing with the Great Depression. Indeed, his first criticism of incumbent president Herbert Hoover centered on Hoover's failure to balance the federal budget. But while uncertain of his agenda, Roosevelt was certain about one conclusion: The national government in Washington, D.C., would be his chief tool in repairing the nation's Depression-struck economy with its collapsed stock market, failing banks, bankrupt businesses and farms, and huge unemployment.

Winning the presidency four successive times, Roosevelt governed primarily by a combination of pragmatic experiments, some of which worked magnificently while others sputtered and failed. Some of his more ambitious programs were nullified by the rulings of a conservative U.S. Supreme Court. Overall, FDR governed as a modern-day American liberal. The New Deal of FDR, which was molded in considerable part by the influence of his remarkable wife, Eleanor, and his diversified "brain trust," became the standard by which liberalism has been judged since 1933.

Throughout my early years in politics beginning in 1953,

Democrats across America, despite the dominant posture and impact of FDR, usually set aside a day marked by annual fund-raising dinners or rallies that were designated as "Jefferson–Jackson Day" events. Republicans had a similar annual observance honoring Lincoln. Both Jefferson and Lincoln have been political heroes of mine, and both, I believe, belong in a quartet of especially great American presidents that includes Woodrow Wilson and Franklin Roosevelt. My den has been adorned over the years with the faces of those four. They are, I believe, the central historical architects of American liberalism. If I were to add two others to my list, they would be Theodore Roosevelt, with his dedication to preserving America's natural heritage, and Lyndon Johnson, with his vision of America as a "Great Society." The tragedy of the Johnson administration lay in Vietnam—a war Johnson did not start but which he failed to terminate and, indeed, greatly escalated. My one reservation with TR centered on his tendency to be overly pugnacious and wild in foreign policy. "I took the Canal and let Congress debate," he boasted in a celebratedly unwise outburst.

Three other faces on my wall—John and Robert Kennedy and Martin Luther King Jr.—were lost to the nation by assassination, a loss beyond measure.

All of these men drew a vital part of their philosophies from the best of American conservatism. That is why I have never been comfortable with being described as totally of the liberal tradition—or, as some of my political critics have put it, "an extreme liberal." I am proud of my liberal heritage, which I regard as the more creative and constructive of our two central political traditions—liberalism and conservatism. But both of these traditions have influenced the presidents I most admire and both have informed and enriched the American nation.

I'm aware that some conservatives regard us liberals as stand-ins for the Antichrist, just as some liberals see conservatives as evil. Both of these views are mistaken. Sean Hannity, the Fox News cohost of *Hannity and Colmes,* is congenial to me on the air and in personal relations, but his most recent book is entitled *Deliver Us from Evil,* with the subtitle *Defeating Terrorism, Despotism, and Liberalism.* What can I say about that—except "No comment"? I'm grateful that Hannity's cohost, Alan Colmes, a strong liberal, has written a much more reasoned book entitled *Red, White and Liberal.* If you want to see me hit the ceiling, just suggest that conservatives are one iota more patriotic than liberals. In World War II I never gave a damn about the political views of the nine men who made up my bomber crew. They were all good men who had volunteered for service in the air war over Europe. They performed their individual tasks well without flinching, and that's why we completed thirty-five tough missions. I did know that my copilot was a conservative Republican, but he flew our B-24 like a bird. I loved him without regard to politics, as I did the other young men in my command. In the years after the war, half of my crew emerged as Democrats and half as Republicans. I love all of them and always will. Every one is a sterling patriot—liberals and conservatives alike. I think they all voted for me in 1972, but who cares? I lost anyway.

Franklin Roosevelt and the New Deal have been the most profound and enduring influences in the shaping of modern-day liberalism. What were the significant achievements of FDR and his New Deal?

It is impossible to contemplate the Roosevelt era apart from the Great Depression, which gave it birth. The disastrous collapse of the stock market in 1929, the earlier bankruptcy of the agricultural economy in 1921, the collapse of the Florida real estate boom, followed by the virtual paralysis of the banking, commercial, and industrial sectors, led to widespread unemployment, business bankruptcies, mortgage foreclosures, bank failures, poverty, and despair. All of these disruptions were exacerbated by the ill-advised Hawley-Smoot Tariff Act (1930), which, to his credit, President Hoover opposed. The tariff greatly aggravated the falling economies of Europe and Japan and in so doing paved the way for the rise of the dictators and World War II.

Neither the incumbent Hoover administration nor its chief ally, the business community, seemed to have any clear sense of what could be done to restore the economy, although Hoover pushed for a worldwide economic conference, which FDR spurned. Roosevelt's landslide win was probably not so much an endorsement of liberalism as it was a rejection of continuing leadership by a hesitant, conservative government and a business community whose practices had seemingly thrown the nation into economic collapse.

The New Deal was Roosevelt's effort to save the capitalistic system from the crisis into which its managers had led it. Similar economic crises had developed in Germany, Japan, and Italy following World War I. Those nations responded by bringing authoritarian dictatorships into power to resurrect their economies—and to set the stage for the most terrifying and calamitous breakdown of international order in human history: World War II.

The Russians, after centuries of misery under the czars, aggravated by their terrible suffering in World War I, turned in desperation to a Communist dictatorship. The British, the French, the Scandinavian countries, and other European governments moved toward democratic socialism.

Roosevelt, a staunch believer in free enterprise capitalism, was not sympathetic to any of these foreign ideological approaches to the economic crisis. He believed throughout his life in the competitive capitalistic system. But he came to the view that this system was being undermined by the excesses of shortsighted, undisciplined entrepreneurs. He was not opposed to businesspeople and investors making a profit, as his father and his extended family had done. Yet he came to deplore the abuses of stock market insiders, unwise banking practices, speculative real estate ventures, and the failure of many business leaders to consider the interests of their employees and the consuming public. Most of all, he, and even more so his wife, found it unacceptable that millions of Americans—men, women, and children—had been bypassed and forgotten by both private business and their government. There were no safety nets for the poor, the elderly, dependent children, unorganized workers, miners toiling in dangerous underground conditions, the handi-capped, small merchants, farmers, the minorities, the illiter-ate or ill-educated, and countless other Americans beyond the reach of a laissez-faire society. In effect, the once pros-perous American economy had ground to a halt and little or nothing was being done to ease the pain of millions of Americans.

Roosevelt found "one-third of a nation ill-housed, ill-clad and ill-fed." He found not only much of the nation's workforce idled, but millions of workers without organiza-tion, representation, collective bargaining rights, or unem-ployment insurance to protect them. He found older people haunted by the specter of insecurity and poverty in the closing years of their lives. He saw hardworking farm fami-lies losing their crops, their markets, their land, and their homes. As farmers lost their purchasing power, main-street businesses also went under. Banks were failing and clos-ing their doors, wiping out the lifetime savings of families, including the six-thousand-dollar, hard-earned, carefully saved accumulation of my own parents. In my home state, South Dakota, and in the surrounding farm states, many of the banks had been closing throughout the 1920s as more and more farmers and businesses went bankrupt.

Roosevelt was determined to act decisively to reduce the impact of the Depression on people's lives.

There was no agreed-upon liberal agenda for FDR to fol-low—no clear-cut alternative to the sincere but ineffec-tive efforts of Herbert Hoover. Theodore Roosevelt and Woodrow Wilson had moved the liberalism of Jefferson and Jackson in new directions. FDR, who had probably given even less thought to forming an overall political philosophy than either TR or Wilson, was ready to try some new practical experiments, with government intervention beyond anything envisioned by Jefferson, Wilson, or his cousin Theodore. Lacking any clear ideological system, he had to move without a defined pattern. His program emerged step by step to form the agenda of liberalism; but by avoiding the ideological terminology of either conservatism or liberalism, FDR gained broad public support as a practical-minded, clever, upbeat, smiling, and confident political leader seeking workable answers to complicated problems.

The British economist John Maynard Keynes presented a political economy that was seized upon by liberals everywhere, including many of FDR's New Dealers and brain-trusters. When a national economy is sluggish and depressed, Keynes called on the government to provide a fiscal stimulus in the form of increased government spending or reduced taxes or both. When an economy is overheated and afflicted by inflation, the remedy is the reverse: less government spending, higher taxes, or both. Why not give these Keynesian theories a chance? FDR reasoned. As he put it during his 1932 campaign: "The country needs and, unless I mistake its temper, the country demands bold, persistent experimentation. It is common sense to take a method and try it. If it fails, admit it frankly and try another. But above all, try something."

Roosevelt borrowed from the ideas of others. He borrowed the regulation of the stock market from Wilson. Theodore Roosevelt inspired his support for the stabilization of agriculture. Senator George Norris guided him in the creation of the Tennessee Valley Authority. For a time, he even borrowed the idea of a balanced budget from Herbert Hoover.

Roosevelt, always the pragmatist, liked to think of the New Deal as free of any ideology. He saw himself simply as a practical problem solver—neither a liberal nor a conservative. Often the target of intense partisan attack from Republicans who had no doubt that he was a confirmed liberal, which, of course, he was, FDR saw himself as a nonpartisan walking cheerfully down the middle of the road, veering neither left nor right.

Assuring the American people "the only thing we have to fear is fear itself," the new president embarked on a New Deal. America's government, its economy, its society, and its standing in the world have all been changed mightily—for the good of humanity.

Chapter 5

THE SOURCES OF SECURITY AND NATIONAL GREATNESS

O, it is excellent
To have a giant's strength; but it is tyrannous
To use it like a giant.

—SHAKESPEARE, *MEASURE FOR MEASURE*

With malice toward none, with charity for all, with firmness
in the right as God gives us to see the right, let us strive on to
finish the work we are in, to bind up the nation's wounds . . .
to do all which may achieve and cherish a just and lasting
peace among ourselves and with all nations.

—LINCOLN'S SECOND INAUGURAL ADDRESS, 1865

I ACCEPT THE PREVAILING VIEW of our political leaders that, considering the terrorist danger, what many citizens most want now is a strong assurance of national security. It is my view that we are not on course toward that increased security. We continue to place too much faith in reducing terrorism by military means and pay not enough attention to other vital ingredients of security. Sending our army into Iraq has weakened the nation's security and increased the terrorist danger while greatly lowering our stature in the eyes of the world. It was, in fact, a costly diversion from the real sources of terrorism.

President George W. Bush made clear in his State of the Union address, January 2004, that he intends to seek reelection on his claim that he has made America more secure. I wish it were true that he has. While I am optimistic about America's future, I believe Mr. Bush's policies have painfully weakened the position of the United States at home and abroad. Every public opinion poll around the globe indicates that the U.S. invasion of Iraq is opposed by the overwhelming majority of the world's people—even in those few countries whose governments or heads of state have endorsed the war. Prime Minister Tony Blair's support for the American war in Iraq has created a serious political crisis in Britain. Beyond this, our economy, our health care, our educational system, our environment, our job prospects, our tax system, our energy system, and our fiscal health are all weaker than they were three years ago when Bush and his party took over the government and then took us into a needless and hopeless war.

Following World War II, the U.S. War Department underwent a name change. With the passage of the National Security Act in 1947, the War Department, by act of Congress, became the Defense Department. At the same time, the term "national security" came into its own as the chief end of the American nation, a concept not mentioned in the founding documents of the country.

What are the real sources of national security?

Of course we need military spending adequate to defend the nation. But excessive arms outlays deplete funds needed for other sources of national power and well-being.

In his eloquent "Cross of Iron" speech, President Eisenhower said: "Every gun that is made, every warship launched, every rocket fired signifies, in the final sense, a theft from those who hunger and are not fed, those who are cold and not clothed. This world in arms is not spending money alone. It is spending the sweat of its laborers, the genius of its scientists and the hope of its children. This is not a way of life at all, in any true sense. Under the cloud of threatening war, it is humanity hanging from a cross of iron."

After his inauguration in 1953, Ike promptly ended our involvement in the Korean War, which had dragged on inconclusively since June 1950. "During the years of my Presidency," he later wrote, "I began to feel more and more uneasiness about the effect on the nation of tremendous peacetime military expenditures. The effects of these expenditures on the nation's economy would be serious . . . their eventual influence on our national life, unless watched by an alert citizenry, could become almost overpowering."

Has an alert citizenry kept a careful eye on the mushrooming arms spending of the last half century? I don't think so.

Have we had thoughtful, courageous political leaders pointing out the military excesses in the federal budget? With few exceptions, I don't think so.

Drawing upon the wisdom of George Washington and Eisenhower and other great American patriots, let us consider the major sources of American strength and national security.

(1) First, our security and national interests are best served by a foreign policy of cooperation and conciliation rather than a confrontational, go-it-alone unilateralism. There may be times when conditions demand a get-tough use of military force, but this should always be a last resort. The Axis dictators—Hitler, Mussolini, and Prime Minister Tojo—presented such a challenge in the 1940s, but even then we wisely conferred and cooperated with our Allies. In managing the foreign policy and defense of the country to advance our security, it is important to remember Jefferson's dictum, "a decent respect to the opinions of mankind."

Powerful states such as ancient Rome, imperial Britain, Hitler's Third Reich, or even the United States of today—which we Americans and many others regard as the world's greatest nation—sometimes have found it easier to overlook the opinions of others. The ancient Romans regarded people beyond their imperial borders as "barbarians." This tendency of preponderant nations was referred to by the late senator William Fulbright as "the arrogance of power." A thoughtful Englishman, Timothy Garton Ash, has more recently observed that "the fundamental problem is that

America today has too much power for anyone's good, including its own." (*The New York Times,* April 9, 2002)

We saw this factor in the recent run-up to the invasion of Iraq. George W. Bush's father, during his presidency, handled preparations for the Gulf War of 1991 masterfully—first gaining approval of the Congress, the United Nations, the European Union, the Arab League, and nearly all the other countries around the globe, including even normally neutral Switzerland and Sweden. Only then did our forces go into battle with help from other countries. Saddam Hussein and his army were quickly expelled from Kuwait, and the war was over in one hundred hours. In the ensuing twelve years, Hussein did not so much as put his big toe beyond his own borders. United Nations weapons inspectors were in Iraq for years to seek out and destroy any strategic weapons. American surveillance planes flew over Iraq daily.

Some critics have said that President Bush Sr. should have ordered our forces to invade Iraq and destroy its government, but the president had no such mandate from Congress, the United Nations, or the nations of the world. The mandate was to drive the Iraqis out of Kuwait, and that is what was done with universal approval. The truth is that nothing more was needed to confine Hussein to his own territory. He was a threat to no other country—least of all the United States.

The current President Bush began by informing both the Congress and the United Nations that while he would like their approval for an invasion of Iraq, he didn't need approval, nor would he delay plans for the war. The Congress did not declare war, nor did the president ask for such a declaration—the procedure of war making required by the Constitution—a requirement ignored not only by Bush and the Congress but by some of the earlier presidents and Congresses. A number of these unconstitutional wars—sometimes popular at the outset—lost public support when they dragged on. When I first spoke out on the Senate floor in 1963 against the American war in Vietnam, polls in South Dakota indicated that 80 percent of my constituents approved of the war.

As a senator first elected in 1962 by a margin of 597 votes after a recount, I continued to speak out against the war, assuming that this dissent would probably make me a one-term senator. But then, public sentiment gradually began to change, and in 1968 I won reelection decisively in the easiest victory of a long career. Four years later, I won the nomination of my party for the presidency in a field of seventeen contenders, including four of my able Senate colleagues: Hubert Humphrey, Ed Muskie, Henry Jackson, and Eugene McCarthy.

It is true that the Congress, months in advance, gave the current President Bush a blank-check resolution to do what he wished, when he wished, with Iraq. The same blank-check tactic gained President Johnson passage of the Gulf of Tonkin Resolution in August 1964. In both of these instances, the Congress was misled by administration officials. The alleged "attack" on two American destroyers by Vietnamese PT boats in the Gulf of Tonkin on August 4, 1964, never took place.

President Bush launched his national security policy in a speech at West Point in May 2002. That September, the

Bush administration issued a comprehensive thirty-three-page report, entitled *The National Security Strategy of the United States of America*. It is a drastic and unwise departure from the assumptions that have guided American policy since World War II. The new foreign policy is said to be largely the creation of the neoconservatives placed in key positions in the Bush hierarchy.

During the long years of the Cold War, neither the Soviet Union nor the United States ever fired a single bullet at the other. They maintained a policy of mutual deterrence and containment, which discouraged aggression by either side. Roughly the same policy was followed toward China after the Korean War. Fortunately, none of the hotheads on either side advocating a preemptive strike against the other ever came to power during the Cold War. Today, we maintain a peaceful policy of diplomacy and trade with Russia and China after a half century of Cold War rivalry.

This same policy of deterrence and containment worked well with Saddam Hussein's Iraq after he was driven out of Kuwait in 1991 by President Bush Sr. and his many allies.

The radical shift in American policy propounded by the Bush "neocons" asserts that America can send its troops into any country that the administration designates as a potential enemy, even though that country has undertaken no military action against us or other nations. The name given to this Bush strategy is "preemptive war"—a fancy phrase for aggression. The current administration gained congressional support for its war against Iraq by claiming that the Iraqis had weapons of mass destruction which they could launch in a few minutes and which, in the words of Presi-

dent Bush, might take the form of a "mushroom cloud"—
shades of Hiroshima and Nagasaki. No such weapons were
launched against our invading troops, nor have our forces
found any such weapons. Neither did the UN arms experts
find these weapons. Their plea for more time to complete
their inspections was rejected by the Bush team.

It was further asserted by Bush spokespeople that Saddam Hussein's Iraq was working with the Al Qaeda network of Osama bin Laden—the architect of the 9/11 attack.
This contention was also false.

And now the president has conceded that there had been
no cooperation between bin Laden and Saddam Hussein. In
fact, the two despise each other, despite the assertions of
administration officials who linked Al Qaeda to Iraq. This
glaring falsehood was concocted by the Bush team to exploit
the trauma of Osama bin Laden's attack of 9/11 as a justification for going after Saddam Hussein. Public opinion
polls indicate that a majority of Americans believed the administration falsehood linking Saddam Hussein to the 9/11
attack. Hussein was bad enough as a dictator without tying
him to an event in which he played no part.

This was the unilateral pattern that prompted the United
Nations to reject the U.S. invasion of Iraq. It also helped
trigger a strong negative reaction from such important nations as France, Germany, India, Russia, and China—all of
whom had supported President Bush Sr. in removing Saddam Hussein's army from Kuwait in 1991.

The current administration's tendency to go it alone
in defiance of international opinion and international law
has been obvious from the beginning. The rejection of the

Kyoto accords on global warming; the decision to scrap the 1972 ABM Treaty and proceed with "Star Wars"; the rejection of the Land Mines Ban and the International War Crimes Court; the continuance of the long-obsolete and self-defeating boycott of Cuba in which America stands alone in the world except for the anti-Castro Cubans in Miami who dictate our policy; the disruption of peace and unification efforts of North and South Korea by cavalierly listing North Korea as part of the "axis of evil"—all of these factors have alienated scores of countries whose goodwill and cooperation we urgently need.

America should be seen in the world as a nation of positive values and reconciliation, not as a bullying giant of confrontation and conflict.

The post-invasion period in Iraq seems to be going badly as it has degenerated into low-level guerrilla warfare with almost daily American casualties. More young Americans have died since the president boldly declared on the deck of an aircraft carrier on May 1, 2003, that the mission was accomplished than were killed before the announcement. The president seemed to enjoy being a passenger while a young naval pilot made a carrier landing off the sunny coast of California. It is the closest he has ever been to war. But the planes, tanks, and artillery ordered by Mr. Bush to hit Iraq claimed an estimated eleven thousand Iraqi lives and left the country without electricity or water from war-damaged public facilities; such damage, along with widespread looting and sabotage of the oil arteries, has caused great public unease and resentment. The Iraqi unemployment level before the war was already high at 40 percent—in considerable part because of the international sanctions; after the taking of Baghdad it stood at 60 percent. As in Vietnam, many Iraqis are sheltering the guerrillas rather than giving information about them to our military forces.

Faced with this unhappy plight, the president belatedly called for UN participation in restoring Iraq and establishing government authority there. In a sense, the administration is being forced to eat crow by admitting that the United States cannot pacify and rebuild Iraq alone.

The president has now told the Congress and the public that the war and recovery costs will be much higher than expected. Also, we have been told that we now need to go back into Afghanistan and finish the costly and difficult reconstruction there following the war of 2001–02. How many more such troubled countries can the United States lay waste and then rebuild?

Having spent roughly $150 billion on the preparations, invasion, and formal war against Iraq, the administration has requested another $87 billion for the current fiscal year and then an additional $25 billion, and this is only the beginning. The Vietnam War cost an estimated $600 billion. We probably will not get off more lightly in Iraq and Afghanistan. No wonder Mr. Bush is crying out to the United Nations and to other nations. The American economy has been shaky for the last three years. Our state and local governments are in financial crisis, and our police and fire departments, schools, and health care are short-changed; our infrastructure of water and sewage lines and our railways and public transit badly need upgrading. Financially, we cannot stand the hemorrhage of more doubtful wars followed by expensive reconstruction. By close consultation and skillful diplomacy, President Bush Sr. persuaded the Japanese and the Saudi Arabians to pay a major part of the cost to force the Iraqi army out of Kuwait. By his go-it-alone attitude and weak diplomacy, Bush Jr. seems to have foreclosed the likelihood of such help from other nations.

After having been proved wrong in its original justification for attacking Iraq—the presence of weapons of mass destruction and the contention that Saddam Hussein was involved in the 9/11 attacks—the Bush administration is now claiming that it invaded Iraq to give the Iraqis democracy. If in fact going to war to deliver democracy was our purpose, we would have to invade half the countries of the world, including some in our own backyard. Democracy is a worthy effort, but that should not be the burden of the American armed forces. It is not easy to export democracy in a B-52 or a tank.

America needs to see itself as part of the global family. It is in our interest to strengthen the United Nations and the World Court. It is in our interest to advocate the development of a UN police force to deal with areas of international conflict. We have veto power over such UN initiatives, but we could well discover that we would use that veto less than is now imagined. Even a wealthy, powerful nation such as the United States cannot alone be the world's policeman, nor should we even covet that unpopular and self-defeating role. That is the mission of the United Nations. Should American troops sometimes be part of a unified international command with some of the officers from other countries? Why not? We did that in World Wars I and II, and in each case we were on the victorious side. American GIs have always enjoyed cussing out their officers; they might enjoy even more cussing out officers from France, Britain, Germany, and Russia. It's a lot more fun to ream out officers from London, Paris, or Moscow than it is guys from Des Moines, Sioux Falls, Albany, Sacramento, or Dallas.

I firmly believe that American security will be advanced by a stronger United Nations, a stronger World Court, a War Crimes Court, an effective international police force, a ban on land mines, and an international, sustained effort to reduce and hopefully eliminate nuclear, biological, and chemical weapons.

My plea for internationalism is complicated by the little understood impact of globalization. Globalization of the international economy seems inevitable. We need, however, to take two important protective steps. Workers in America must be protected against runaway corporations seeking cheap labor and bad working conditions in poor countries. We haven't even begun to solve this problem, nor is there an easy answer. Until an answer is found, we have a right to close American markets to this unacceptable undercutting of jobs and wages in the United States. We should insist that our trading partners maintain wages in some reasonable relationship to wages in the United States.

The second challenge of globalization is to protect Americans from corporations that go abroad to evade environmental standards. There are solutions to this problem, as there are to the labor standards difficulty, but it will require hardheaded, tough leadership by our government to achieve those solutions. We should press for international environmental standards instead of rebuffing such international goals, as we did in walking out on the Kyoto accords. The United States should be in the lead seeking to protect its citizens with fair labor and environmental standards. If we solve these two challenges, globalization might become an important factor in drawing nations into closer cooperation.

(2) The wise use of our food production to end hunger in America and reduce it abroad is not only a humanitarian act, it advances our national security. I have long believed that a national commitment to end world hunger would greatly strengthen both American foreign policy and our agricultural economy.

For most of my adult life I have had a special concern for hungry people—especially children—in the United States and around the world. Perhaps this concern began in childhood and youth when I saw South Dakota farmers and ranchers toiling and sweating not only from planting and harvesting but from their battles with drought, dust storms, grasshoppers, and wind storms. If victory was achieved over these obstacles in the growing season, our agricultural and livestock producers would often then see the market break under the pressure of farm surpluses.

Yet when I went to Sunday school and religious services at the little Wesleyan Methodist church in my neighborhood, the teachers and the minister would ask us to pray and give to starving people in Armenia, China, India, Africa, and elsewhere, including the poor of America.

Farmers going broke as surplus crops depressed their markets while multitudes of people went hungry is a cruel paradox I have sought to resolve for half a century.

In the late summer of 1944, I was on a troopship with hundreds of my fellow bomber pilots and our crews as we approached the Italian harbor of Naples, ready for combat. It was a bright, sun-filled day, and alongside the docking area we could see a large gathering of children who seemed to be shouting at us. As the ship moved closer, we could make out their cries in broken English: "Hey, Joe, Butterfingers, Hershey Bars, Babe Ruths. Hey, Joe, Wrigley's gum!"

At this point, the captain of the ship announced over the loudspeaker: "Do not throw anything to the children. This is wartime Italy. Those children are near starvation. Yesterday an American ship docked here and the sailors threw candy. Some of it fell in the sea and several children drowned trying to retrieve it."

After we encamped in army tents on the Adriatic coast and began flying bombing missions over Nazi Germany, we would sometimes see young Italian women in the morning, scratching through our garbage area to find scraps of food for their children. In some instances we would see the same women in the evening, selling themselves on the streets to gain a few dollars for their families. More than one American serviceman rationalized this exchange of dollars for romance on the grounds that he was thereby feeding the hungry—while satisfying his own lonely inner needs. It is not clear that this was the appropriate interpretation of the admonition of Ecclesiastes: "Cast thy bread upon the waters for thou shalt find it after many days."

That grim and dangerous year in Italy was eye-opening. It gave me my first clear look at the tragedy of human hunger. Of course, today Italy is among the best-fed nations in the world. But warfare and destruction ravished the Italian countryside, its soldiers, and its people. I have never been able to put those gaunt, hungry faces out of my mind's eye.

By the time I completed thirty-five combat missions and was thereby qualified to return home to the United States, the war in Europe suddenly ended. But the commanding officer of the 15th Air Force, General Nathan Twining, asked pilots to stay in Italy a little longer and fly American bombers loaded with food we no longer needed to war-torn countries of Europe. I volunteered for this service—my first experience in feeding people, sometimes the same people we had been bombing a few days earlier. That was an inspired way to end service as a combat pilot in Europe.

Fifteen years later, in 1960, after two terms as a South Dakota congressman, I was appointed by President John Kennedy to be the first U.S. Food for Peace director. That challenging opportunity gave me the chance to direct the shipment of millions of tons of American surplus grain to the hungry people of Asia, Africa, and Latin America. We shipped 4 million tons of surplus American grain annually to India alone. These shipments, plus edible oils and additional farm produce from the United States, literally kept the Indian people alive in the critical 1960s.

The wonders of the "Green Revolution," in which American scientists, most notably the Nobel Prize–winning Norman Borlaug, showed the farmers of India, Mexico, and other developing countries how to apply science to the improvement of seeds and cultivation of crops, converted India into a grain-exporting country. This does not mean that India is free from hunger. There are still millions too poor to buy the food they need even when it is available from their own producers. But Dr. Borlaug and his associates have greatly advanced the development of India and other countries.

In 1968, CBS aired an hour-long television documentary, *Hunger USA.* I watched this brilliant program in amazement. It documented graphically the existence of malnutrition and hunger in large pockets across America—migrant labor fields, urban slums, impoverished and abandoned mining towns, struggling rural areas, and Indian reservations.

But the scene that most gripped my heart was a little boy standing in a southern school lunchroom watching his classmates eat. When the reporter asked him what he was thinking, he lowered his head, dug his toe into the floor, and said softly, "I'm ashamed."

"Why are you ashamed?" asked the reporter.

"Because," said the boy, "I haven't got any money."

I said to one of my daughters sitting with me in our comfortable Washington home, "It's not that little youngster who should be ashamed. I should be ashamed as a U.S. senator who didn't even know that children who can't afford it are not provided a school lunch." These were the children most likely to have trudged off to school after a makeshift breakfast. Children can't learn effectively under these conditions. They tend to become life's losers.

So I went to the Senate the next day and introduced a

resolution calling for the creation of a Senate Select Committee on Nutrition and Human Needs. That resolution, bolstered by the drama of the CBS report, was approved without serious opposition.

As the chairman of the committee for the next decade, I worked closely in a nonpartisan manner with Senator Robert Dole to transform the nation's food assistance programs and the nutritional health of all Americans. We provided free or reduced-price school lunches for children from low-income families. We tripled the Food Stamp program. We launched a new program known as WIC (women, infants, and children), which provides nutritional supplements to low-income pregnant and nursing women and their infants through the age of five years.

No one can fully estimate the contributions of these food assistance programs as investments in the well-being and security of American families.

In 1997, President Bill Clinton appointed me as U.S. ambassador to the United Nations Food and Agriculture Organization in Rome. This appointment, which I held for four years before being named by the UN World Food Program as ambassador on global hunger, enabled me to develop a school lunch program that I hope will eventually reach every elementary school child in the world not now being offered a daily school lunch.

My friend and former Senate colleague Bob Dole has joined me in this effort. This may become the most important initiative I have undertaken in a long life of striving to end hunger in the world. It will feed 300 million children every day when fully implemented.

What could this mean to the world and to America's international standing?

1. Careful studies of pilot school lunch programs in developing countries leave no doubt that they pull children into school. As matters now stand, of the 300 million targeted elementary school students, 130 million—mostly girls—are not attending school. But when a good school lunch program is started, both girls and boys flock to the schoolroom.

2. The second result is that academic performance improves when children break the school day for a nutritious lunch. Improved nutritional health means increased productivity and creativity.

3. The third result is remarkable. Whereas illiterate girls with no schooling marry as early as age ten, eleven, or twelve and have an average of six children, girls with six years of schooling marry later in life and have an average of 2.9 children. Thus, girls drawn into school by the prospect of a good meal cut the birth rate in half without resorting to abortion. This result is the product of education.

I'm convinced that the tools of nutrition and education in the hands of the United Nations and voluntary private agencies, with the United States in the lead, provide an instrument that can diminish the anger and terrorist impulses of many young people in the world.

President Clinton launched U.S. participation in this global effort by providing $300 million in American funds. We have had strong bipartisan support in the Congress and some support from the Bush administration. More support is needed—not only from our government but from other countries, wealthy individuals, corporations, and foundations.

One aspect of the issue of human hunger that has long appealed to me as a practical politician is that this is clearly a soluble problem. Human conflict may not be soluble. Human beings have been killing one another with increasing intensity ever since the days of Cain and Abel. The twentieth century was by far the bloodiest and most violent in the long history of the human race. But hunger is a political problem that can be resolved in the next twenty-five years if we and others dedicate ourselves to that goal. The universal school lunch program, combined with an international WIC program, could cut in half the 800 million chronically hungry people in the world by the year 2015. It is entirely possible to end the hunger of the remaining people by the year 2030. Food should be the right of every human being—especially children—an announced goal of our foreign policy and an important stone in our national security edifice. Unquestionably, it will strengthen America's foreign relations and our posture in the world.

As Gandhi put it, "To a hungry child, God can only appear as bread." I suspect there would be less terrorism and more peace in the world if American foreign policy borrowed more of Gandhi and less of Caesar. Remember, the Roman Empire declined and fell, whereas Gandhi drove the mighty British Empire out of India by nonviolent, peaceful means. Stalin once asked contemptuously: "How many divisions does the pope have?" The answer is: Enough to survive for two thousand years, unlike Stalin and all the other dictators before him who have disappeared from history.

No other goal of my public life has claimed more time and energy than feeding the hungry at home and abroad, both by sharing our agricultural abundance and by teaching the farmers of a struggling world how to be better farmers and better stewards of God's earth, seas, and skies. I have trudged through hundreds of poor, dusty villages in Africa, Asia, Latin America, and the Middle East—usually with an interpreter to help me converse with the people in their homes, on their farms, in workplaces, and on the streets. In some villages I have watched children leaning over mud puddles that served some of the time as latrines, cupping their hands and drinking filthy water. Most of the widespread infectious diseases that kill young and old alike stem from unsanitary water, unwashed hands, and undernourished bodies, minds, and souls.

Suppose that instead of invading Iraq, the United States had persuaded the United Nations to join us in providing a good, nutritious school lunch every day to every schoolchild in Iraq. All of this could be done under the experienced guidance and monitoring of the UN World Food Program and our philanthropic and religious voluntary private agencies. The World Food Program was directed during the decade of the 1990s by a superb, tough-minded American woman, Catherine Bertini, appointed by the senior President Bush. The agency is now directed by an equally dedicated business executive named by the current President Bush, James Morris of Indiana. This program could be supplemented by one of the most successful American food assistance achievements, WIC, which provides nutritional supplements to women and their small children.

Does anyone doubt that America's approval rating would go up as word of such practical, lifesaving food assistance programs spread from Iraq across the Arab world and around the globe? Governor Tom Ridge, who now heads the Homeland Security Department, warned that an American invasion of Iraq would likely trigger more terrorist attacks against our people. Whether in Iraq, Israel, Palestine, Afghanistan, or elsewhere, war begets more terrorism, not less. On both a humanitarian basis and grounds of hard-headed reality, it makes more sense to feed the children than it does to blow apart an ancient civilization along the Tigris and Euphrates rivers that has been around for five thousand years.

America will be safer in the feeding business than in the war business, and we will sleep better at night—the sleep of the just. We might even soften the hearts and reduce the anti-Americanism of the bitter young men who fill the ranks of Osama bin Laden's Al Qaeda.

In any event, this is the course that draws on the best traditions of America, in Lincoln's words, "the better angels of our nature." This is, as Herbert Agar wrote, "A Time for Greatness." It is immoral to watch a child die every five seconds from hunger while we have more food than we can consume or sell.

And so it goes with other issues that we face. Every one of them has a crucial moral component. It is immoral to pollute the air, water, and soil of God's creation. It is immoral to permit a fifth of America's children to grow up in poverty. One of my most thoughtful European friends told me that no government in Europe could escape collapse if it were revealed that a fifth of their children were living below the poverty line. It is immoral for 800 million of the world's people to be hungry from birth to death. We and other nations know how to end that hunger, and at modest cost. All the religions of the world command their adherents to feed the hungry.

I believe that the kind of cooperative, compassionate foreign policy I have suggested is a most important step on the way to national security and to doing the will of the Almighty.

(3) Another source of national security is a healthy American citizenry. There are some things that a person learns just by growing older. Having reached the eighty marker, I have learned that next to a clear conscience, the most important asset one can have is good health. If an individual is afflicted with heart disease, stroke, high blood pressure, liver damage, arthritis, emphysema, Alzheimer's, clinical depression, alcoholism, or other serious ailments, life loses much of its joy and satisfaction. Ill health also curtails the productivity

and creative capacity of the victim, which in turn weakens our society and our security.

Although I grew up in the Great Depression, my parents used their meager resources to provide good medical care for our family. During my years as an Army Air Corps bomber pilot in World War II, I received superb physical training, a balanced diet, and excellent medical care. Since then, my earning power, although modest, has been sufficient to cover the cost of medical insurance. Twenty-eight years of government service has expanded my health insurance and medical attention. In short, I have benefited from excellent medical coverage all of my long years.

I owe my years of public service in war and peace in considerable part to the high energy and mental and physical toughness that derives from good health. With the exception of a period of deep depression that followed the tragic death of my third daughter, Terry, I have suffered no serious illness. Even in this one instance, superb medical care at Johns Hopkins University Hospital returned me to good health. When I left the U.S. Army Air Corps in 1945, every fiber of my 165 pounds was as hard as steel. I'm no longer that tough, but I still weigh 165, work ten hours a day, and only rarely experience even a minor illness. (Knock on wood.)

Unfortunately, many of my fellow Americans have never experienced the kind of medical attention lavished on me. They struggle through life burdened by depression, alcoholism, malnutrition, asthma, headaches, heart problems, respiratory ailments—and the list goes on. Forty-four million Americans cannot afford health insurance. The nation is obviously weakened by this neglect of health considerations.

During World War II, Congress was shocked to learn that one of every three young Americans reporting for military service had to be declared physically ineligible—many of them because of childhood malnutrition—especially young men who had grown up in the South.

These uncomfortable conditions prompted Georgia senator Richard Russell, chairman of the Senate Armed Services Committee, to introduce the first federal school lunch program.

But what of the potential Dwight Eisenhowers, John Kennedys, Martin Luther Kings, César Chávezes, Gloria Steinems, Elizabeth Doles, and Shirley MacLaines who never matured into greatness because of medical neglect and ill health?

What can we do for those who can't afford health care? I suggest the following simple formula:

Extend Medicare to all Americans now six years of age and under. After two years, extend Medicare from age seven through eighteen. After another two years, extend the program to ages nineteen through thirty-five. After two more years, extend it to those thirty-six through sixty-four.

This formula has the advantage of extending an existing program that the Congress, the press, the medical establishment, and the public are all familiar with—health insurance for those sixty-five and over. There would seem to be no reason why this same benefit should not apply to those Americans under sixty-five.

Congressman Richard Gephardt has come up with an imaginative formula for financing health insurance for those Americans now without coverage. He would cancel the administration's $2 trillion tax reduction for our wealthiest citizens over the next ten years and instead use these funds to finance health care—a vital building block in national security. Our richest citizens would probably enjoy life more if, instead of a tax gift they don't need, they were enabled to use that money to provide health insurance for their low-income brothers and sisters.

(4) The fourth building block of national security is education. Our forefathers understood this elemental truth from the beginning. Just six years after the Pilgrims landed on the rocky shores of New England to found the Massachusetts Bay Colony, Harvard College opened its doors to "train young men in the Christian religion."

As the tide of settlement moved down the coast from Massachusetts to Georgia, other colleges opened their doors. Everywhere settlers went in the New World, they built schoolhouses, churches, and sometimes libraries. In every village, town, and city—and throughout the rural areas in between—the schoolhouse was a vital center of education, learning, and civic pride.

The great Northwest Ordinance of 1787 set aside vast acreages of public lands to nourish and strengthen the public schools. The Morrill Act of 1862 provided federal land grants to enable each state to have a College of Agriculture and Mechanical Arts.

The National Defense Education Act enacted by Congress in the 1950s provided low-cost government-guaranteed loans for college students. This legislation has an interesting history, which I know well as a member of the House Education Subcommittee that drafted the bill. The measure grew out of the launching of the first space vehicle by the Soviet Union in 1957, which was dubbed "Sputnik." This unexpected launching prompted American political, military, and scientific leaders to wonder if the Soviets were ahead of us in scientific studies. The first draft of the student loan bill limited its benefits only to students majoring in science. As a former history professor, I argued that the federal government should not discriminate against students majoring in history, government, economics, literature, and other subjects important for the nation's security and well-being. My motion to open up the program to all students carried and became part of the bill.

Prior to the passage of this initiative, other efforts in the 1950s to provide federal aid to the schools had all failed. Such measures were blocked either by southerners who feared amendments that would force an end to racial segregation, or by conservatives across the country who worried about the cost of the program and possible federal meddling in local school matters.

How to get around these concerns? We found the answer in the title we assigned to the bill—the National Defense Education Act. We were convinced that few members of Congress would vote against a bill carrying the label "National Defense." Our strategy worked to perfection: the bill sailed through the House and Senate, and a beaming President Eisenhower signed it into law—education for national defense.

One of the most remarkable educational initiatives ever pursued by the federal government was the G.I. Bill of Rights following World War II. Sixteen million young Americans who participated in that conflict were given the opportunity to go to any college of their choice and receive a degree—all at government expense, plus a monthly stipend covering living expenses.

That public investment educated millions of young Americans who went on to become engineers, lawyers, doctors, professors, congressmen, military officers, clergy, journalists, bankers, musicians, writers, and all the other professions. In my case, the measure enabled me to care for my wife and two children while going through Northwestern University to a Ph.D. in history.

Tom Brokaw has labeled my generation "the greatest generation." If we deserve that lofty phrase, it is because of three factors: the Great Depression and World War II, which honed and strengthened us, and the G.I. Bill of Rights, which educated and refined us.

The G.I. Bill cost the government a great deal of money, while enriching our colleges and the GI students. But reputable studies have concluded that the federal government made money on its education investment. It did so by increasing the earning power of the GIs, which in turn produced higher income tax revenues from the veterans for the rest of their lives.

Now is a good time to revive the G.I. Bill formula, but it should be open to all Americans who wish to extend their education. With unemployment at the highest level in many years, why not offer these idle people and others a chance to go to college or vocational school to pursue the course that most appeals to them? As was the case with the G.I. Bill, they would need a cost-of-living stipend. Such an opportunity would seem to appeal especially to the thousands of workers caught up in the downsizing of many corporations.

I am not an economist, but I believe that just as the original G.I. Bill generated more revenue for the U.S. Treasury than the cost of the program, so could it be with a revival of that formula.

Today, our elementary and secondary schools are in financial crisis. State and local governments are facing funding problems across the land. Some states have no income tax or sales tax; they depend almost exclusively on property taxes for revenue. But even wealthy states with broad-based tax systems such as California, New York, Florida, and Texas are in financial crisis and unable to strengthen their schools.

What is needed is a return to the states and municipalities of some of the federal revenues collected across the nation. This revenue sharing should be large enough to ensure quality education in every state. I will explain later how this investment in education for the security and well-being of the nation can be financed without an increase in either taxes or the national debt. Clearly, an educated citizenry is essential to the security and quality of our society, the growth of our economy, and our national defense. A healthy, educated citizenry must take priority over any other foundational stones for a democratic society and a dependable national defense.

• • •

(5) A fifth foundation stone of national security is our richly endowed physical environment—clean air, clean water, fertile soil, healthy forests, user-friendly public parks and recreation areas. Our marvelous national parks and forests are the nation's crown jewels.

We will add greatly to the preservation of the environment if we develop such clean renewable sources of energy as hydrogen, solar, and wind power. One low-cost step in this direction would be to go back a hundred years to when every farm had a windmill to pump water and generate electric power.

Developing renewable clean sources of fuel and energy is clearly an improvement in national security in that it will reduce our dependence on the foreign sources of oil located in sometimes turbulent and unstable areas of the globe.

Global warming is not a myth. Some of our greatest scientists have been warning of calamitous repercussions as the atmosphere heats up due to polluting gases around the world—especially over such highly industrialized countries as the United States, Western Europe, Russia, Japan, and China. We can reduce pollution and improve our transportation choices if we upgrade and extend our railways both for passenger service and for the shipment of heavy goods. A century and a half ago, America pioneered the building of great railroads. We should have the best, safest, and swiftest railway system in the world. The alternative is more cars, trucks, and buses on our highways, with more pollution, more congestion, and more accidents.

Building and operating a national railway system could provide good jobs for America's unemployed, as would upgrading our urban transit systems.

When I recall my years in World War II, I think of going back and forth across the country on trains from one military base to another. I don't know how America could have prevailed in either World War I or World War II without its railway system. But that system has been deteriorating ever since. It now needs to be completely rebuilt, with state-of-the-art rails, signals, communications, engines, and cars.

One important step forward for all Americans is to move ahead on a modern energy policy embracing hydrogen, nuclear, solar, wind, and ethanol power. Senator Tom Daschle of South Dakota, my longtime friend, has legislation pending to achieve a modern energy policy. If we make the proper use of our own fuel sources, our leaders might not be so quick to send our army into the oil-rich states of the Middle East.

These steps to safeguard our environment, improve our energy uses, and strengthen our transportation system can contribute mightily to our national strength.

(6) From the earliest days of the republic, an invaluable source of American security and well-being has been the amazing agricultural production capacity of the nation's farm families. With the exception of freedom itself, no other resource has contributed more to the strength and health of the nation than our independent farmers and ranchers. No

other country in human history has equaled the record of American farmers in feeding the population with such a small fraction of total consumer spending. The typical family across America has more than enough to eat, with a smaller percentage of the family budget devoted to food, 18 percent, than any other nation on the planet.

During the long Cold War rivalry between Moscow and Washington (1945–90), the United States was able to maintain military superiority over the Soviet Union by allocating the major portion of the federal budget to military purposes. The Soviets tried to match our armed strength by devoting an even greater percentage of their smaller national budget to armaments. Moscow was never able to match the U.S. military strength, but it remained a powerful competitor in the force of its arms—especially in defensive capability, including the huge Red Army with its tanks and heavy artillery.

In the vitally important area of agriculture, the USSR's collective farms were never any match for America's independent family farms. During this critical period of rivalry between the two superpowers, America's farm families, making up 5 percent of our population, each produced enough food to feed thirty-nine other people. By contrast, the USSR's farmers, who constituted half the population, had difficulty in feeding the other half of their people. Farming involves such difficult labor and management that it requires the work and skills of an interested owner to achieve maximum productivity and careful conservation of the land. Collective farming seems better in theory than it proved to be in practice. If human beings were saints, they might work as efficiently in collaboration as they do individually, but alas, we seldom achieve sainthood.

No one understood the magic of America's farm production better than the wily Russian leader Nikita Khrushchev. When he accepted an invitation from President Dwight Eisenhower to visit the United States in the late 1950s, he expressed no interest in visiting American military bases, as suggested by his host. "We have missiles and planes," he said. Instead, Khrushchev asked to see two of America's marvels—an Iowa corn farm and Disneyland. No missiles or bombers, thank you. Let me see something important. Mickey Mouse and a cornfield. The Secret Service said no to Mickey Mouse. Too many security risks at Disneyland. And that was before the Terminator took charge in California! But they said Khrushchev would be safe in an Iowa cornfield unless some South Dakota pheasant or deer hunter wandered across the border.

Having grown up as a peasant, Khrushchev knew well the hardship of life on the farm, especially during the long, dreary Russian winters. He also knew about the miracle of American farm production, as did Mikhail Gorbachev—the Russian minister of agriculture, later to become the president of the Soviet Union who negotiated an end to the Cold War with Ronald Reagan.

Beyond maintaining America's food supply, the major factor in America's international balance of trade has been our agricultural exports. Were it not for the farmers who feed us, with enough left over to supply a huge commercial export market, we would be faced with a calamitous imbalance of trade, our dollars and gold drained all over the planet.

We have marvelous industrial and technical resources in the United States. But other countries can match us in the production and export of cars, machinery, steel, photo equipment, electronics, shoes, clothing, furniture, and ships. In the industrial sector, we run a negative trade balance. For many years we have relied on the farmer to make us competitive in global markets and to prevent our trade imbalance from getting worse than it already is.

It is the American farmer who also makes possible our vital food assistance programs at home and abroad—the federal school lunch program, the WIC program, Food Stamps, Food for Peace, and the UN World Food Program.

From the beginning, our best leaders have recognized the crucial role of U.S. food producers. Thomas Jefferson observed that "cultivators of the earth are the most valuable citizens." In numerous writings Jefferson made clear his strong belief that the vitality of American democracy, the moral fiber of the nation, and the health of our economy depended in considerable part upon the preservation of the independent family farms. "The small landholder is the most precious part of the state," he asserted. He worried over the prospect that rural Americans would be swallowed by urbanization, Americans "piled upon one another in large cities."

Abraham Lincoln, perhaps our greatest president, shared Jefferson's devotion to rural America. Indeed, Lincoln as president signed into law three landmark contributions to U.S. agriculture—all of them in 1862, at the height of the

Civil War, when the war was going badly for the Union forces. The first of these measures was the Homestead Act, which opened up the frontier to family-type farming based on 160-acre homesteads for each farmer willing to work the land. This was the formation of the American family farm. The second was the Morrill Act, which brought into being the land-grant college system, with its programs of agricultural research and education followed by experiment stations and extension services that have greatly enriched the lives of rural Americans. The third measure of that crucial year was the creation of the U.S. Department of Agriculture, which by 1960—a century later—had become the second biggest federal department, exceeded only by the Department of Defense. Its services to rural America now include research, conservation, price supports, marketing, loans for purchase and operation of farms, food safety, nutrition, rural electrification, and telephone services.

The nation has wisely supported these three crucial building blocks of the agriculture edifice for more than a century.

In Jefferson's day, the first American census, held in 1790, classified 94 percent of the population as rural. The census of 1900 indicated that only 38 percent of Americans were rural dwellers. By 1965, that figure had declined to 8 percent. Today, only 4 percent of the American population is classified as rural. But so great is the productivity of America's farm families that the 4 percent who reside on farms are able to feed the 96 percent who reside in the towns, cities, and suburbs of the United States.

Indeed, so great is the output of America's farms that surpluses regularly pile up and depress the prices and income of farm families. As a lifetime student of agricultural issues with twenty years of service on the U.S. House and Senate Agriculture Committees, I am grieved to witness how hard farmers work and how little they often receive for their produce. As matters now stand, the nation is losing large numbers of farmers who can't continue farming because of low farm prices with rising farm costs. Family-size farms are being swallowed by larger landowners and merged into corporate-size units. Beyond this, millions of acres of productive farmland are being taken over by swelling city suburbs, golf courses, airports, industrial parks, and roadways. This is a trend that not only drives up the cost of farmland to young families wanting to become farmers, it also replaces the beneficial farming green belts around our cities with concrete and smokestacks and disrupts the biodiversity and wildlife of the land around our cities.

I believe there are answers to these problems. The problem of farm prices and incomes being driven down by surplus production can best be solved by reviving the "ever normal granary and parity" formula devised by Secretary of Agriculture Henry Wallace during the New Deal of the 1930s. Under this formula, farmers would be guaranteed a fair price—90 percent of parity—for their produce if they agreed to idle some of their land. This would have the effect of protecting farm prices while also encouraging the conservation of land that would be allowed to lie idle for periods of time.

Farmers guaranteed a fair price for their produce would not be forced to give up their farms, which would benefit them and the nation by preserving our farmland and our food supply. This price-support system should be limited to family-size farms. The larger farm operators can do well without price-support subsidies because of the economy of large-scale production.

We must not only create jobs for our unemployed urban workers, we must save the right to farm of every farm family in America. The farms of America from Maine to California and from Florida to Oregon are vital to our national security and the health of our economy.

We can constructively use some of our surplus farm commodities by reaching more of the world's 800 million chronically hungry people. The international school lunch program supported by former senator Robert Dole and me and by Congressman James McGovern and Congresswoman JoAnn Emmerson, which was launched by President Clinton in 2000 with an initial grant of $300 million in farm commodities, is now rightly regarded by Mr. Clinton as one of his brightest achievements. The program has been authorized by Congress with broad bipartisan approval and is supported, however weakly, by the Bush administration. It now enhances the World Food Program, which is reaching 16 million children in thirty-eight countries.

Other countries should and probably will contribute to this effort. With 280 million elementary school children yet to be fed a daily lunch, we could help both these hungry youngsters and our farmers by substantially increasing our contribution through the UN World Food Program and the voluntary philanthropic and religious overseas agencies. These agencies include CARE, Catholic Relief Services, the Land O'Lakes Corporation, Church World Service, Lutheran World Relief, the Jewish Distribution Committee, the American Friends, the Mennonites, and others. The United Nations and the private agencies are now efficiently providing a good nutritional school lunch every day for nearly 20 million children. Many of these recipients are being reached as the result of the McGovern-Dole initiative launched by President Clinton. Much of this is made possible by the surplus production of U.S. family farms. But much more can be done to the benefit both of our farmers and of the hungry children of Africa, Asia, Latin America, and the Middle East.

Farmers and their small-town neighbors have even deeper concerns than their urban cousins about available health care, quality schools, and jobs for the members of their families. Farm families are worried about the seemingly unchecked and unregulated growth of agribusinesses and corporate agriculture. They also fear the impact of globalization and the complicated new trading systems.

Don Morrison, director of the North Dakota Progressive Coalition, contends that "there are two places in America where you see the most pain, the most economic injustice: the inner city and rural America." Many Americans, including numerous economists, believe that the Great Depression began with the collapse of the stock market in 1929. It actually began with the collapse of the agricultural economy throughout the 1920s—1920 to 1930 and beyond.

John Nichols points out that the prosperity of the 1990s never reached most of rural America. During that decade, 676 of the nation's 3,141 counties lost population, and the worst population losses were in what is still referred to as America's heartland. "More than 60 percent of the counties in the Great Plains have experienced depopulation." (*The Nation,* November 3, 2003)

People are not leaving the farms of America because they dislike the rural life; they leave because they can't achieve a living income. With our cities overcrowded, plagued by unemployment, with schools and other public institutions strained, it behooves us to support stronger income incentives, with better health and educational opportunities for those who create the nation's food production.

As matters now stand, some of our best farmland is being taken away by urban sprawl—unchecked and unplanned. This is a threat both to would-be farm families and to the cities that depend on them for food. At present, 86 percent of our vegetables and fruits are grown and 63 percent of our dairy products are produced on prime farmland around our cities—Billings, Sioux Falls, Fargo, Minneapolis-St. Paul, Omaha, Des Moines, Chicago, Denver, Los Angeles, New York City, St. Louis, Atlanta, New Orleans, and Seattle. These rich farming belts also shelter wildlife and provide scenic beauty around our urban areas. Yet this is the land being gobbled up by developers in an unplanned way for non-farm uses, without regard to the impact on the environment, the wildlife, the scenic beauty, and the nation's food supply. With farm prices too low and farm costs rising, farm families are selling off their land to the developers.

We are now losing 1.2 million productive acres of farmland annually to sprawling development with insufficient attention to the needs of both cities and rural areas. This means that each year we are forfeiting an area of good farmland equal to the state of Delaware. Scattered development of this kind around our cities increases taxes and strains costly public services, causing more traffic congestion, more water pollution, a loss of wildlife, and less conservation of the soil.

A private nonprofit organization, the American Farmland Trust, is providing part of the answer to this national problem by buying up threatened farmland and selling it back to would-be farmers with an agricultural conservation easement that restricts its use to farming. Beyond this, what is needed is a commitment by cities, states, and the federal government to add support, both in land-use planning and by financial investment in preserving farmland, with special attention to the land around our cities. Every American has a personal stake in keeping our farmers and ranchers on their land and in making our central cities more habitable for those residents who now flee the cities for new housing in the country. Every level of government has a stake in the protection of our precious food-producing farmland. This is a matter vital to our national security and to our health and well-being as a society. Jefferson and Lincoln knew what they were about when they honored the American family homestead. When we lose our family farmers, we do so at our peril.

(7) The seventh source of national security is a credible federal government. Our leaders and our candidates for high office simply must speak the truth as they honestly see it. The credibility of government and the faith of the people

in their government are essential ingredients of our willingness to defend the nation against enemies, foreign and domestic.

In World War II, during my days as a combat bomber pilot, I lived in a small tent with the three other officers on my bomber crew. The other pilots and their crews were encamped close around us in the olive trees and vineyard terrain outside Cerignola. We ate, drank, smoked, caroused, and flew together. Never once do I recall any morale problem, despite the danger and loss of pilots and crews on missions over Nazi Germany. Nor do I recall any aspersions cast against our government in Washington. It never occurred to me to question the integrity of the White House, the Department of State, or the War Department. Perhaps this was true in part because we were young and naive. But I think the central reason for our respect of the government is that we were not lied to and we believed in the stated goals of the war and the hopes for peace.

During the ill-fated American war in Vietnam, I visited the battlefronts three times as a U.S. senator, beginning with a Thanksgiving visit in 1965. My son-in-law Wilbur Mead was then a Marine based with General Lew Walt's 3rd Marine Division at Chulai, near Da Nang. On each of these visits I talked at length with our fighting men and their officers in the combat zones, in their camps, in the hospitals, and on the streets of Saigon—including an overnight visit with General Walt. I found a growing number of men on each visit who were demoralized, confused as to the war's objectives, and doubtful about the reliability of their government.

One of our best officers in Vietnam was General Creighton Abrams, with whom I had a lengthy visit in Saigon. He knew that I had long been a critic of American involvement in Vietnam, but he spoke with me in complete candor. When I asked him about his progress against the Vietcong guerrillas, he replied: "Senator, the Vietcong are a problem, but there are other problems that worry me more. I worry about my demoralized troops. I worry about desertion. I worry about so many of my troops hooked on drugs. I worry about all the guys who are suffering from venereal diseases. I think we might be able to handle the Vietcong if it weren't for all these other hindrances."

The soldiers in Vietnam knew about the "credibility gap" that plagued the Johnson administration and then the Nixon administration that followed. They also knew that this painful "gap" was a product of the Vietnam disaster. They were to learn later about the Watergate scandals that deposed President Nixon—scandals that developed in considerable part from the administration's obsession with Vietnam.

The only oath a president or a senator takes is to uphold the Constitution. If that oath had been kept, there might have been no Vietnam War, no Watergate, no Irangate, and no invasion of Iraq.

In the absence of faithfulness to the Constitution and to basic morality, we will continue to have credibility gaps, loss of faith in our leadership, and reluctance on the part of both our soldiers and our citizens to give their full support to the government.

There is one long-overdue step that we must take in the interest of a Congress and a presidency capable of serving the public's well-being. That step is to replace private interest money in financing political campaigns with public money. As matters now stand, both the Congress and the White House are under the heavy influence of huge sums of money given by wealthy citizens or special interests. This is not to suggest that elected officials are taking bribes; it is to say that congresspeople and presidents are not as free as they should be from political pressures that are not always in the public interest. Also, the present situation compels elected officials to devote upward of a third of their working days to raising money for the next election.

I would like to see legislation enacted that would prevent the expenditure of any private funds in congressional or presidential elections. The federal government should set reasonable spending limits and then provide the same amount of funds for the opposing candidates.

The best way for taxpayers to protect themselves is to invest a modest portion of their taxes in financing clean elections.

We Americans have benefited from some great leaders in our history—George Washington, Thomas Jefferson, Abraham Lincoln, Woodrow Wilson, Franklin Roosevelt, to name a few. My constant prayer for America is that such leaders will serve us again. A credible government with dedicated leaders is essential to our national security.

(8) The eighth and final ingredient of national security is our military strength. We need an efficient, well-trained,

well-equipped Army, Navy, Air Force, and Marine Corps. America today has the best military forces in the world. We can continue our superior military forces with a considerable reduction in arms spending, which can be diverted to other ingredients of national power and security.

I do not suggest any cuts that would weaken our security. But neither do I want to see military spending that goes beyond our defense needs, because I believe such spending weakens the nation. It does so by needlessly increasing taxes, raising the national debt, and absorbing public funds needed for other parts of national security such as health, education, transportation, and the environment.

I have proposed a 5 percent reduction in the next year's military spending, with the savings invested in other sources of national strength that are now painfully underfunded.

One need not be a military expert to know that U.S. military spending in excess of all the rest of the world is far beyond what is needed to turn back any aggressor nation or any combination of nations.

No country now threatens the United States; therefore, we should be able to reduce military spending by 5 percent annually until it reaches $250 billion—still far and away the biggest military budget on the planet. This should give us a leaner, tougher, and more efficient military force. It will also free up nearly $250 billion for other vital parts of our national defense, including education and a modern, state-of-the-art railway system.

I'm assuming that having blundered into Iraq—a country that posed no threat to America and had nothing to do with the 9/11 catastrophe—we will not soon plunge into another debacle in violation of our Constitution, international law, and common sense. We have to begin showing more concern for our troops, who will be dying in Iraq indefinitely, as they did in Vietnam for many years. It is hypocritical to consign our young soldiers to needless wars in Vietnam, Iraq, and elsewhere and then fill our store windows with signs reading SUPPORT OUR TROOPS. Let's really support our troops by keeping them safely at home with their families rather than dispatching them abroad under the cockeyed notion of what our president has called "preemptive war"—a concept previously recognized as aggression, a violation both of our Constitution and of international law. The Japanese tried to wage "preemptive war" by sinking our fleet at Pearl Harbor. Hitler waged preemptive war against Europe and the United States. They both failed, and their leaders were convicted of war crimes. Mr. Bush would be well advised to consign his preemptive war theory to the ashcan of history.

The British Conservative member of Parliament, Edmund Burke, had it right: "A conscientious man would be cautious how he dealt in blood."

There is, of course, the terrorist danger. But terrorism is not a military problem, nor can it have a military solution. The nineteen young followers of Osama bin Laden who destroyed the World Trade Center and a section of the Pentagon were not armed. Carrying only pocket-size plastic box cutters, they hijacked four civilian airliners, and the rest is history. The point is that battleships, tanks, missiles, artillery, and submarines are useless in combating terrorism.

What is needed against terrorists is good local police and fire departments—the heroes of 9/11. It is also important for the president to order the CIA and the FBI to start talking to each other and to share pertinent information with state and municipal law enforcement people. Our law agents had enough information to have avoided the 9/11 attack if they had only shared what they knew or if superior officials had acted on reports from their field officers.

I recognize that the trauma following the 9/11 attack demanded an American response. But I think the reaction of the current administration has been misdirected.

We of course need to take some precautions at our airports, perhaps arming the pilot and copilot on commercial airplanes with grapeshot guns and putting a similarly armed marshal on each flight. But the army of inspectors, searchers, police officials, and soldiers who now clutter up our airports, requiring passengers to empty their pockets, take off their shoes and belts, and wait in line while their baggage is searched—all of this is dubious. When I walk into an airport, I don't fear a terrorist attack—I fear the delay and frustration of trying to survive all the barriers before I finally fall into my seat, flustered and exhausted, or sometimes even missing my flight.

One fact is certain: No one will ever again be able to hijack an airliner by brandishing a box cutter. It worked on 9/11 because at that time airline crews were under instructions not to resist hijackers. But since 9/11, any would-be hijacker waving a little box cutter would either be laughed at or knocked out by a punch in the nose from the pilot or copilot or a kick in the crotch by a flight attendant. I'm eighty-one years old, but I have no fear of doing battle with some character threatening me with a box cutter. What sets my teeth on edge is seeing a frail little aging woman trying to get her shoes off to be searched, lest she slip by with some trinket that could endanger the republic.

The measures I have proposed in this chapter will cost some money—for ending world hunger and for health care, education, the environment and modern railroads. Where will that money come from? It will come from the peace dividend I have proposed—$25 billion each year for ten years—and it will come from canceling the Bush $2 trillion tax cut over the next decade, which is largely for the rich who least need a tax cut.

Chapter Six

COME HOME, AMERICA

The mystic chords of memory, stretching from every battlefield and patriot grave to every living heart and hearthstone all over this broad land, will yet swell the chorus of the Union, when again touched, as surely they will be, by the better angels of our nature.

—LINCOLN'S FIRST INAUGURAL ADDRESS

I LEARNED OF THE World Trade Center disaster while having lunch with editors of the *International Herald Tribune* in Paris. As the American ambassador to the UN Food and Agriculture Organization in Rome, I was leaving that day on a mission to Africa to evaluate the malnutrition and AIDS epidemic on that besieged continent. Immediately, in France, Italy, and other European states and across Africa, there was an outpouring of sympathy and support for America. French diplomats and government officials I conferred with before continuing on my mission to Africa were struggling with tearful responses. The next day a leading French newspaper carried a headline: "We Are Now All Americans."

Regretfully, that genuine outpouring of sympathy from Paris to Tokyo, Rome to Moscow, Jerusalem to Johannesburg, Sydney to Mexico City, was thrown away by the Bush strategists. I can think of no other period in American history when our politics, our policies, and our diplomacy so quickly converted the goodwill of the world into outright resentment and fear of the American colossus. Most of the anti-American sentiment that swept the world stemmed from Mr. Bush's bullying, unilateral invasion of Iraq in defiance of the United Nations and international opinion everywhere. Exceptions were the British prime minister and a few other heads of state. In each case, public opinion polls in those countries indicated that the citizenry was strongly against our war in Iraq. America has been left standing virtually alone as far as the people of the rest of the world are concerned.

A key fact is that almost no one believes Iraq had anything to do with the 9/11 attack. And they are right about that, as President Bush now concedes. That being the case, how could an American president have sent young Americans to die in Iraq instead of concentrating on the real sources of danger to America, especially Osama bin Laden?

Beyond this, the president has asserted a new doctrine alien to America's tradition and to international law: "preemptive war." There has never been a day when I was unwilling to risk my life in defense of this country that has given me so much. But neither God nor man has endowed our nation with the right to declare that every other nation must see things as we do or else accept our right to attack them. You are either for us or against us, Mr. Bush asserts to the entire world.

Well, Mr. Bush, I'm for America, but I'm not for your policies. I'm for our troops, but I'm not for their commander in chief, who sent these brave young men and women to attack a country that has done nothing against us and poses no threat to our security.

As for the Patriot Act, supported by the administration and enacted by Congress, this measure is not only completely unnecessary, it is a contradiction of the Bill of Rights. It gives Washington the right to snoop into our mail, our reading matter, our medical records, our bank accounts, purchases, loans, and mortgages, along with many other aspects of our personal privacy. Any of the feds who attempt this with me will get a hard shove out the door. I'll go to jail rather than accept such an invasion of my freedom as an American. But I don't want to go to jail; hence my advice that Congress repeal the misnamed Patriot Act, which should have been called the Anti–Bill of Rights Act. I especially reject the idea of a witch doctor such as John Ashcroft deciding what qualifies us as patriots and traitors. This is the Alien and Sedition Acts revisited.

George Washington believed that the love of freedom and devotion to our country sprang from our inner beings and did not require regimentation of the governed. In his superb farewell address, he said: "Interwoven as is the love of liberty with every ligament of your hearts, no recommendation of mine is necessary to fortify or confirm the attachment."

Congress could warm the souls of Washington, Jefferson, and Lincoln if it took a careful look at this hastily drafted measure to legislate patriotism and then repealed it.

Nor do we need the huge new federal bureaucracy known as Homeland Security. With its 200,000 employees and a budget of $30 billion annually, this agency has all the earmarks of a white elephant or a beached whale. Governor Ridge is said to be a very able man, and doubtless he is. But why ask a good man to waste his time and talent trying to orchestrate twenty-two government agencies rolled into one department? The purpose of all of this was to get the agencies with some involvement in counterterrorism under the same roof, on the theory they would then share information and skills with one another. But 9/11 revealed that the two agencies that most need to talk to each other and share their information are the CIA and the FBI. Guess what? The CIA and the FBI are excluded from the Department of Homeland Security.

I have a suggestion, now that our judgment and common sense may be a little stronger than they were immediately after the 9/11 trauma. Let's get rid of all the barricades and hassles of passengers at our airports. And then, with thanks to the Patriot Act for making us patriotic and equal thanks to the Homeland Security Act for making us secure, let us arrange a proper funeral for these two monstrosities.

Of course, what I'm really trying to say is that the Patriot Act will not make us patriotic and the Homeland Security Department will not make us secure.

Perhaps we need to hear again the words of Benjamin Franklin in 1759: "Those who would give up essential liberty to purchase a little temporary safety deserve neither liberty nor safety." And we might well listen to the more recent words of Senator Hillary Clinton, speaking on January 24, 2003, at John Jay College of Criminal Justice: "We have relied on a myth of homeland security, a myth written in rhetoric, inadequate resources, and a new bureaucracy, instead of relying on good old-fashioned American ingenuity, might and muscle."

Fundamentally, the answer to terrorism is to root out its causes. Why are young men willing to die striking a blow against the United States? One reason, I repeat, is that these men—some of whom are educated—view the hunger and poverty of much of the Arab world against the background of America's wealth and lavish lifestyles. They see their own joblessness and helplessness—if not hopelessness—against America's enormous military and financial power. And they are furious.

Historically, the poor in the city slums and the peasants who work the land have always hated the rich guy in the big house on the hill. America is now the rich guy on the hill— richer than anybody else, more powerful than anybody else, and sometimes more arrogant than anybody else. And to the Arabs, we are the guy in bed with the Israelis while we position our troops and bombers on Arab lands. This is a formula for the kind of anti-Americanism that fuels the terrorist danger.

Osama bin Laden devoted most of the 1980s to fighting with the Taliban in Afghanistan against Russia's occupying force. When he returned to his home in Saudi Arabia, he was furious to find half a million American troops quartered in his country with the approval of his king and his own prominent, wealthy family. Having driven 100,000 Russian "infidels" out of Afghanistan, he was now confronted with five times that many American "infidels" in his own country—the keeper and protector of the holiest of holy Islamic cities, Mecca and Medina.

His rage as a Muslim zealot against the United States and his own government knew no bounds. Denouncing the Saudi king and his own family, he went back to Afghanistan reportedly with a parting family gift of $400 million. He then began the series of bombings of two American embassies in Africa, the USS *Cole* off Yemen, and the two symbols of American financial and military power—the World Trade Center and the Pentagon. A fourth plane that crashed in the Pennsylvania countryside after a struggle between a hijacker and the passengers and crew was apparently headed for either the White House or the Capitol.

A perceived affront to their religion and national honor by the presence of American forces in their lands is doubtless one factor in arousing the terrorists. Before we dismiss that concern too lightly, let us recall that one of the stated grievances of the American colonies that drove their revolutionary war against Britain was the quartering of British troops in the American colonies.

Another factor in Middle East anger against the United States is America's longtime close alliance with Israel. Without debating the merits of that alliance, which I have always supported, we should face the reality that it has long complicated our relationship to the Arab world. It does not go down well for our leaders to hammer any Arab or Muslim state that considers building a nuclear facility, while remaining silent about Israel's nuclear weapons. President Bush Sr. and his secretary of state, James Baker III, understood the problem and worked diligently to pursue a more even-handed U.S. policy in the Middle East. Presidents Carter and Clinton also tried to be fair to both Arabs and Israelis. More needs to be done in this direction in concrete ways. The culmination of the Clinton mediation was a meeting at the White House in which Yasser Arafat, the Palestinian leader, and Yitzhak Rabin, the Israeli prime minister, shook hands and pledged to find a peaceful solution. But after his return to Israel, Mr. Rabin was assassinated by a crazed Israeli religious fanatic—a staggering blow to Middle East peace.

We can only hope that President Bush and his secretary of state, Colin Powell, will be able to revive peace talks in the Middle East as they have attempted to do. A just peace between Israel and the Palestinians will go a long way to reducing some of the anti-American emotions that now drive the terrorist impulse.

Avraham Burg, the distinguished Speaker of Israel's Knesset from 1999 to 2003, writing in the Israeli journal *Yediot Aharonot* early in 2004, courageously spelled out the conditions of a just peace: "We cannot keep a Palestinian majority under an Israeli boot and at the same time think ourselves the only democracy in the Middle East. . . . We must remove all of the settlements and draw an internationally recognized border between the Israeli national home and the Palestinian national home."

During a recent visit to Detroit, I was told by a group of thoughtful Arab Americans whom I have long respected that if America could broker a fair peace settlement between Israel and the Palestinians, this would do more to end the terrorist danger from the Middle East than any other step we could take. These were professional people—doctors, lawyers, teachers—who carry no malice toward either Israel or the United States.

As Avraham Burg put it to his fellow Israelis: "It is not a matter of Labor versus Likud or right versus left, but of right versus wrong, acceptable versus unacceptable. The law-abiding versus the lawbreakers." And then, directing his attention outward, Mr. Burg added: "Israel's friends abroad—Jewish and non-Jewish alike, presidents and prime ministers, rabbis and lay people—should choose as well. They must reach out and help Israel to navigate the road map toward our nation's destiny as a light unto the nations and a society of peace, justice, and equality."

Jimmy Carter, our Nobel Prize–winning former president and author of the Camp David accords resulting in a lasting peace between Israel and Egypt, has long held convictions similar to Mr. Burg's.

Consider what a refreshing change it would be for the world if the Middle East cauldron of barbed-wire entanglements, suicide bombers, tanks, and helicopter gunships could be replaced by two ancient peoples living side by side along recognized boundaries and sharing the glory of Jerusalem—the vision of Avraham Burg and the Arab Americans of Detroit.

It would also reduce much of the Arab friction toward

America if we withdrew our troops from Saudi Arabia and other parts of the Middle East. This is the kind of concrete, visible step that will ease anger toward America and thus reduce the danger of terrorism.

Unfortunately for America, for Israel, and for the Palestinians—indeed, unfortunately for the peace of the world—there is an influential group of advisers in the current administration who do not want an even-handed American role in resolving the Arab-Israeli conflict. This group of neoconservatives includes Deputy Secretary of Defense Paul Wolfowitz, advisers Richard Perle, Douglas Feith, Ken Adelman, and others. Among the views of the neocons, none is more deeply held than their belief that the United States should always support the government of Israel no matter what policy that government pursues. To the neocons, it is acceptable to criticize the American government, but to criticize Israeli policy is seen as anti-Semitism. This, of course, is the reason why almost no American politician who covets elective office will ever take issue with Israeli policy.

The irony of the neoconservatives' policy designed to help Israel is that their strategy may be the greatest threat to Israel, in that it feeds an increasingly dangerous Arab-Israeli conflict. Peace can be achieved only if both the Israelis and the Palestinians abandon their bloody reprisals against each other. America can best advance a settlement that will benefit both sides by opposing the belligerent policies of General Sharon and the suicide bombers of Palestine. The provocative militarism of the Sharon administration is a suicidal policy for Israel. No true friend of Israel should support such a self-defeating policy.

Beyond their total commitment to Israeli policies, the neocons are the chief architects of the ill-advised American invasion of Iraq. They are also behind the unfortunate "axis of evil" speech in which President Bush identified Iran, Iraq, and North Korea as probable future targets of American military might. Such warmongering is beneath the dignity of a great nation. It may have caused a spurt of activity by North Korea and Iran to achieve nuclear weapons as a deterrent to an American attack.

The neocons were doubtless as aware as many of us that Iraq had no weapons of mass destruction to pose a threat to the United States. They surely knew that the Iraqis had nothing to do with the 9/11 tragedy. So why did they press for an American invasion of Iraq? I believe they did so because they wanted to establish an American-sponsored political, economic, and military bastion in the heart of the Middle East. Such an American presence would be capable of neutralizing or destroying Arab states and militant bands that posed a threat to Israel and possibly to the U.S. interest in Middle East oil. There have been numerous leaks to the media from the Bush team indicating plans for possible future attacks on such Arab or Muslim states as Iran, Syria, Lebanon, Libya, Yemen, and Somalia. We can only hope that the unforeseen complications now unfolding in Iraq may give our policymakers pause in launching additional wars in the Middle East.

There is one potentially calamitous danger to America from terrorists that may be more serious than any the administration has yet addressed. This is the danger that one or more of the chemical or nuclear facilities across our own country could be breached by a well-planned attack.

The General Accounting Office (GAO) reports that "123 chemical facilities located throughout the nation have toxic 'worst-case' scenarios where more than a million people in the surrounding area could be at risk of exposure to a cloud of toxic gas if a release occurred." The GAO finds that if disrupted, 700 other plants could threaten at least 100,000 people in the vicinity of each plant, and another 3,000 plants could each endanger at least 10,000 people.

Anne-Marie Cusac, an investigative reporter for *The Progressive* magazine, has looked into this potential danger and reports that the Bush administration is aware of it but has not used its authority to insist on safety steps at the plants because private industry opposes any government intervention that might cost it money in providing safety measures.

As far back as February 6, 2000, CIA director George Tenet testified that Al Qaeda could be planning to target chemical plants. The following year, the Bush administration announced that terrorists might be planning attacks on our "nuclear/chemical industrial infrastructure."

Yet the administration backs away from requiring plant managers to take commonsense safety measures that private industry opposes.

Former senator Gary Hart of Colorado, an expert on these matters, contends that there has been no leadership at the White House or in the new Department of Homeland Security to make our chemical facilities safer. And adds Senator Jon Corzine of New Jersey: "The Administration is putting the interests of industry ahead of the safety of the American people."

While serving as head of the Environmental Protection Agency, Christine Todd Whitman drew up plans to require chemical plants to take needed safety steps. But her proposals were killed at the White House after lobbying groups, including the American Petroleum Institute, went into action. The Bush team permitted corporate greed to win over national security.

If the administration is truly interested in preventing a future terrorist attack far more destructive than 9/11, it will move now to secure our chemical and nuclear plants even if it means offending some of its big corporate backers.

A second danger largely ignored by the Bush administration is that containers on ships arriving in New York City, Philadelphia, Boston, Baltimore, Charleston, New Orleans, Los Angeles, Seattle, and elsewhere are not properly inspected for explosive devices. The potential danger here is far greater than at any of our airports. These maritime shipping containers could easily carry chemical or nuclear devices capable of wiping out an entire port city. Many of the inspectors now assigned to our airports should be reassigned to our ports.

More than a decade ago, in 1992, a distinguished medical doctor and scientist at the State University of New York, Steven Jonas, wrote a book entitled *The New Americanism*. In this valuable work, Dr. Jonas said: "We are what we are because of the grandeur of the thought, writing and meaning of our Founding Fathers. If we return to their concepts, and only if we return to their concepts, we can overcome the difficult obstacles that face us."

I have agreed for many years with this broad analysis. Two decades earlier, 1972, the rallying cry of my presidential campaign was "Come Home, America." This was a call for America to return to the ideals of the founders—the Declaration of Independence and the Constitution with its Bill of Rights—and to the latter-day convictions of Abraham Lincoln and others.

I believe deep in my soul that the wisdom, spirituality, and common sense of our founders can best guide the American ship of state. This remarkable group of men led us to independence and freedom, preserved the Union, and gave us the greatest Constitution in human history—a document that opens with this enduring statement of national purpose: "To . . . establish Justice, insure domestic Tranquillity, provide for the common defence, promote the general Welfare, and secure the Blessings of Liberty to ourselves and our Posterity."

A people inspired by these founding principles and served by a constitutional government will do more than anything else to elevate America's standing in the eyes of the world and to promote the well-being and security of the nation.

Looking back on what I have written here about complex problems and potential solutions, I wonder if I have been sufficiently humble. Some of the difficulties that face us—

human conflict, for example—have been around for ages. They don't lend themselves to quick and easy solutions. Some are so rooted in past mistakes that a positive outcome is now difficult to chart.

Pondering the invasion of Iraq under the doctrine of "preemptive war" and wondering how we can now honorably extricate ourselves from that unfortunate venture, I recall the old story of a traveler who crossed into Illinois one evening. Noticing a bystander on the street, he asked him for directions to Peoria.

"If I was going to Peoria," said the resident, "I sure as hell wouldn't begin from here." But here is where we are. And we need both courage and humility in the quest for Peoria.

I have argued that the surest guide to finding our way to Peoria, or Kalamazoo or San Antonio or Vancouver—or even Pumpkin Center, South Dakota—is to consider the wit and wisdom of our founders, their devotion to truth, their sense of history, their respect for human dignity, their humor, and their reverence for the moral and spiritual truths of God's universe.

Of course, the founding fathers would recognize that individuals of humble origin and low station in life often have an abiding common sense that we should draw upon. "Many are in high place, and of renown: but mysteries are revealed unto the meek," the Scriptures tell us.

Euripides wrote: "Humility, a sense of reverence before the sons of heaven—of all the prizes that a mortal man might win, these, I say, are wisest; these are best."

I can only hope that the thoughts and suggestions offered

in this book are leavened by an appropriate mixture of humility and "reverence before the sons of heaven."

Our president told us during the campaign leading to his disputed election in 2000 that he was a "compassionate conservative." I cannot see how his record since then has been either compassionate or conservative. What does compassion mean? It means, I think, a capacity for mercy and concern toward our fellow humans and toward "all creatures, great and small." It means a special concern and kindness toward those who are too young or too old to care for themselves. It means a passion for justice in a sometimes unjust society. At times, compassionate people have been referred to derisively as "bleeding heart liberals." I don't mind that label. Sometimes our hearts should bleed for the children of the world who die by the thousands from hunger every day. And our hearts should bleed for gallant young men and women dying in battle. My heart was bleeding and broken over a daughter who died from alcoholism at Christmastime in the snow of Wisconsin.

Compassionate people are at their best when they are tough-minded but tenderhearted. Lincoln was a man of tough mind and tender heart. Once, during the Civil War, a group of women waiting to see the president heard him laughing. The spokesperson for the women told Lincoln that she was bothered by his laughter, given the tragic nature of the war. Lincoln's reply: "Ma'am, if I could not laugh from time to time, my heart would break."

Franklin Roosevelt frequently found humor and laughter even in the war years of his presidency. But America's poor, its workers, farmers, and small merchants, the elderly, sick, and homeless saw a man of deep compassion smiling at them with his cigarette holder cocked at a jaunty angle.

Roget's Thesaurus likens "compassionate" to "tender-hearted," "benevolent," "humane," "kindhearted," "responsive," "humanitarian." The Apocrypha of the Greek Bible offers this passage: "For the Lord is full of compassion and mercy, long-suffering and forgiveth sins, and saveth in time of affliction."

There is a school of thought in American politics that holds that the mark of a good leader is hardness and toughness—if not outright ruthlessness. Adherents of this view reserve a certain contempt for individuals of compassion and tender hearts.

I have sometimes wondered if the display of toughness is not compensation for uncertainty about one's masculinity. In the case of tough women, is this an effort to demonstrate that women can be as hard and mean as their male counterparts?

During the years of Senate debate over the war in Vietnam, it frequently seemed to me that the most savage war hawks were those who had never experienced war themselves. It's easy to be brave and militant with someone else's blood. For a few of my Senate colleagues who seemed to love the massive U.S. bombing of the Vietnamese, I had reason to believe those fierce armchair warriors had been careful to avoid any actual combat for themselves. The louder the war cries, the weaker the combat experience.

Frequently, on the Senate floor or on the political hustings, the tough guys implied that people of compassion were softheaded—unable to recognize reality. Responding to these implications, Minnesota's great liberal senator Hubert Humphrey asserted: "Compassion is not weakness, and concern for the unfortunate is not socialism."

Condoleezza Rice, the president's national security adviser, is a well-educated, articulate, competent woman with whom I have had a congenial relationship. I heard her speaking on television to the student body of Texas A&M some months ago, when one of the young men in her audience asked her what has been accomplished to make us safer from another Al Qaeda attack. She replied that the administration has been engaged in "the hardening of America." Perhaps I've gone soft in my older years, but I don't like to accept anything called the "hardening" of this land I love more than life itself.

The America I believe in and fought for in the skies over Europe in World War II is a nation with a big heart and an inspired vision. I'll remember always the report Wendell Willkie made to President Roosevelt after a globe-circling tour at the dawn of that second world conflict. Willkie, a liberal-minded Indiana businessman, was Roosevelt's opponent in the election of 1940—the strongest contender Roosevelt faced in his four presidential elections. In his report, *One World*—the most widely published book of the war years—Willkie wrote that everywhere he went around the world, the greatest power and influence of the United States rested on the admiration and affection people had for this country.

President Roosevelt shared Willkie's view. He had earlier launched the "Good Neighbor" policy toward Latin

America. He pursued a system of reciprocal trade with other nations. He laid the foundations of the United Nations. He was regarded around the world as a magnanimous, far-sighted statesman.

I find it sad that the worldwide goodwill the United States commanded in 1940 has vanished. What has happened? Why is the United States regarded in recent international polling as the nation posing the greatest threat to peace?

There is strong evidence that President Bush's announced policy of "preemptive war" is part of the problem. There is nothing in international law or the canons of decency that authorizes a nation to attack another nation on the doubtful grounds of a possible future threat. Not one person in ten in scores of populations polled believes that Iraq, even with Saddam Hussein, constituted a threat to the United States.

What makes matters worse is that the Bush doctrine can just as logically be used to invade other nations our president decides to target.

It is painful to me as an American, rather well traveled abroad, to be told by foreign journalists, teachers, politicians, writers, and clergy that they see America as a bully bent upon a go-it-alone approach in the world. Having identified Iraq, Iran, and North Korea as an "axis of evil," the president told the world that he would not hesitate to attack these nations or any others that might be harboring terrorists. "You are either for us or against us," the president tells the world.

I cannot buy that picture of America. It may stir the

macho spirit in some, but I see it as a pale substitute for "America, the beautiful." Such warmongering and saber rattling is a threat to young American life—and a cloud over this "sweet land of liberty." Great American diplomats such as Benjamin Franklin and Thomas Jefferson were admired and loved by the French, the British, and other Europeans as our ambassadors to those lands. Nearly two centuries later, as a special assistant to President Kennedy and his Food for Peace director, I recall the warmth that the people of Europe, Latin America, Africa, and Asia had for John Kennedy's America. "Where have all the flowers gone?" asks the ballad of the 1960s. Where has all the goodwill gone? Where do we go from here?

Faced with the crisis of the Great Depression, FDR was uncertain how to proceed. Yet he said: "It is common sense to take a method and try it. If it fails, admit it frankly and try another. But above all, try something." Today no one knows for sure what will work best at home and abroad. But our present condition demands change; so let us be about that task.

I think that America can rebuild the goodwill of the world, but not by preemptive war and not by turning our backs on the Kyoto Protocol, the War Crimes Court, the ban on land mines, and the proliferation of nuclear weapons. The United Nations sits on American soil on the banks of New York's East River. It desperately cries out for American leadership and cooperation rather than rebuffs and unilateralism. We can rebuild the goodwill lost on the East River if we truly return to Franklin Roosevelt's dream.

I also believe that if the United States will press the UN

and the voluntary support agencies to provide a daily school lunch for the 300 million children not now being fed, this will transform life on our planet, including the international standing of America. This is the kind of work that makes us stand tall—taller than killing people, even people who irritate us and won't always do what we want them to do.

Finally, we will stand taller in the world if we clean up our politics, safeguard our environment, build better railroads, put our unemployed back to work, provide universal health care, and strengthen education.

How do we do all of this? Remember the words of our founders: "A decent respect to the opinions of mankind"; "Life, Liberty and the pursuit of Happiness"; "government of the people, by the people, for the people." And most important, let's appeal "to the better angels of our nature." Come home, America, to the ideals that guided us in the beginning.

IN CONCLUSION

O N July 13, 1972, in Miami, Florida, I accepted the Democratic nomination for the presidency. Perhaps the closing lines of my acceptance address in the early-morning hours of that long night would be an appropriate ending for this book written thirty-two years later:

> We are not content with things as they are. We reject the view of those who say: "America—love it or leave it." We reply: "Let us change America, so we can love it the more."
>
> And this is the time. It is the time for this land to become again a witness to the world for what is noble and just in human affairs. It is the time to live more with faith and less with fear—with an abiding confidence that can sweep away the strongest barriers between us and teach us that we truly are brothers and sisters.
>
> So join with me in this campaign. Lend me your strength and your support—and together, we will call America home to the ideals that nourished us in the beginning.

From secrecy, and deception in high places, come home, America.

From a conflict in Indochina which maims our ideals as well as our soldiers, come home, America.

From military spending so wasteful that it weakens our nation, come home, America.

From the entrenchment of special privilege and tax favoritism—

From the waste of idle hands to the joy of useful labor—

From the prejudice of race and sex—

From the loneliness of the aging poor and the despair of the neglected sick, come home, America.

Come home to the affirmation that we have a dream.

Come home to the conviction that we can move our country forward.

Come home to the belief that we can seek a newer world.

And let us be joyful in the homecoming. For:

"This land is your land, this land is my land.

"From California to the New York Island,

"From the redwood forests to the Gulf Stream waters.

"This land was made for you and me."

May God grant us the wisdom to cherish this good land and to meet the great challenge that beckons us home.

This is the time.

ACKNOWLEDGMENTS

SIX GREAT TEACHERS, all deceased, have had much to do with any merits of this book: Rose Hofner, my high school English literature teacher; Bob Pearson, my high school American history teacher and debate coach; Don McAninch, my philosophy professor at Dakota Wesleyan; and three graduate school professors of history at Northwestern University, Ray Billington, Leften Stavrianos, and Arthur Link. My debt to these teachers is beyond measure.

I'm also indebted to Arthur Schlesinger Jr., Ken Galbraith, and Gloria Steinem for many years of long and stimulating conversation—and to the late Steve Ambrose, who encouraged me to write this book.

What can I say about David Rosenthal and Alice Mayhew of Simon & Schuster other than to acknowledge that they are the best in publishing and editing? And my warm thanks to editor Roger Labrie for his careful reading and improvement of the manuscript.

And thanks to my agent, Esther Newberg, who made all of this possible with a profit to all of us.

INDEX

Abrams, Creighton, 139
Adams, John, 3, 5, 47, 63
Afghanistan, 15, 19, 20, 108, 149–50
Africa, 17, 145–46
Agar, Herbert, 14, 18, 119
agriculture, 41–42, 93, 96, 111,
    128–37
    see also farmers
AIDS, 16, 145
Aiken, George, 25, 61
Air Force, U.S., 35–36, 55, 141
airport security, 18, 143–44, 148,
    156
Alien and Sedition Acts (1798), 47,
    147
Al Qaeda, 14–16, 23, 106, 119, 155,
    161
anti-Americanism, 16–18, 119, 146,
    149, 151
Anti-Ballistic Missile (ABM)
    Treaty, 17, 107
anti-Communism, 45, 48, 49
Arafat, Yasser, 20, 151
armaments industry, 45, 51, 52, 55,
    62, 72
Army, U.S., 35–36, 55, 141
"axis of evil," 21, 35, 107, 154, 162

balanced budget, federal, 50, 90, 97
balance of trade, 130–31
bank failures, 90, 93, 95
Bible, 5, 6, 8, 11, 158, 160
bin Laden, Osama, 14–15, 19, 20,
    106, 119, 142, 146, 149–50

birth rate, reduction of, 116
Borlaug, Norman, 113–14
Brands, H. W., 65, 68, 75
Bryan, William Jennings, 84–85
Burg, Avraham, 151, 152
Bush, George H. W., 12, 27, 58,
    62–63, 119, 151
    Gulf War and, 27, 103, 105, 106,
    109
Bush, George W., 15, 20, 25, 26, 30,
    59, 60, 68, 100, 119, 144
    "axis of evil" concept of, 21, 35,
    107, 154, 162
    conservatism of, 75–76, 159–60
    national security policy of,
    104–5, 155–56
    preemptive war policy of, 18,
    105, 142, 146–47, 158, 162
    school lunch programs and, 117,
    134
    unilateralist foreign policy of,
    17–19, 25, 102–11, 146–47
    see also Iraq, invasion of
business interests, 80, 81, 83–85,
    86–90, 93, 94–95
    see also corporations

campaign finance, 140
Carter, Jimmy, 5, 26, 27, 64, 67, 151,
    152
Central Intelligence Agency (CIA),
    24, 46, 71, 143, 148, 155
child nutrition, 50, 61, 115, 119,
    122

Index

Index

Index

Index

Index

Index

Index

ABOUT THE AUTHOR

GEORGE MCGOVERN was a U.S. senator for South Dakota from 1963 to 1981 and the Democratic Party's candidate for president in 1972, when he lost to the incumbent, Richard Nixon. He served in the U.S. House of Representatives from 1957 to 1961, when he became the first director of the U.S. Food for Peace Program under President John F. Kennedy. A bomber pilot decorated with the Distinguished Flying Cross in World War II, he was awarded the Presidential Medal of Freedom in 2000. He holds a Ph.D. in history from Northwestern University and served as the U.S. Permanent Representative to the UN's Food and Agriculture Organization under President Clinton. He divides his time between South Dakota, Montana, and Florida.